WHO DARES WINS

WHO DARES WINS

Peter Legge
with
Duncan Holmes

EAGLET PUBLISHING

Eaglet Publishing
4th Floor, 4180 Lougheed Highway
Burnaby, British Columbia, V5C 6A7 Canada

**National Library of Canada
Cataloguing in Publication Data**

Legge, Peter, 1942-
  Who dares wins

ISBN 0-9695447-1-5

  1. Success. 2. Self-actualization (Psychology). I. Holmes,
Duncan. II. Title.
BF637.S8L454 2001   158'.1   C2001-910199-6

First Printing   April 2001
Second Printing   May 2002

Jacket design by Catherine Mullaly
Typeset by Ina Bowerbank
Edited by Kim Mah
Printed and bound in Canada by Friesen Printers

Other books written by the author:

How to Soar With The Eagles
You Can If You Believe You Can
It Begins With A Dream
If Only I'd Said That

Dedicated to
My parents Winnifred and Bernie Legge
who taught me the importance
of developing one's character.
Who always loved and trusted me.
Who dared to come to Canada
for a new and exciting life
and in every conceivable way won!

I miss you both and love you beyond words.

And to my wife Kay and three daughters,
Samantha, Rebecca, and Amanda.
Who have inspired me to be all that I can.
I could not be more blessed
as a husband or father.

To my mentors with deep appreciation

Raymond J. Addington, O.B.E.
Former President of Kelly Douglas & Co. Ltd.

Dr. Mel Cooper, C.M., O.B.C., L.L.D. (HON.)
Chairman & CEO, CFAX Radio

Dr. Joseph Segal, C.M., O.B.C., L.L.D. (HON.)
President of Kingswood Capital Corporation

Acknowledgements

AT THE BEGINNING of my first book, "How to Soar With the Eagles," published almost a decade ago, I said that my life had been influenced by many people whose words, thoughts and actions had made me listen, think, and sometimes move in a new direction. Others, I said, had given me powerful, life-long encouragement and inspiration.

At the beginning of this, my fifth book, I can say the same thing. This too is a book about people and their achievements, whose stories have touched my life, and changed it for the better.

Putting a book together is always a team effort, and I have worked with the best. Once again Vancouver writer **Duncan Holmes** put my thoughts into words. Duncan has an uncanny way of understanding where I want to go, and an amazing ability to add touches that make messages memorable. He is a skilled craftsman and a good friend.

There are others. **Janice Maxwell**, my executive assistant, continues to keep my business life, my speaking life and my charity life on track, and her contribution in a project of this kind is indispensable. **Kim Mah**, the Best Proofreader in the West, dotted the Is and crossed the Ts. **Cathy Mullaly**, the skilled Senior Art Director at Canada Wide, designed the cover. **Ina Bowerbank**, Typesetter Extraordinaire, did just that. **Corinne Smith**, our amazing Production Manager at Canada Wide, insisted that we stay on schedule, and we did.

I thank **Peter Ladner** of *Business in Vancouver* for his

generous permission to quote freely for our **Morris Wosk** chapter.

I thank all of the extraordinary people we have featured in this book, whose lives and good works have inspired me.

And again, my special thanks to **Roberto Lammam**, the genial host at Dario's La Piazza Ristorante at Vancouver's Italian Cultural Centre, where for many months Duncan and I ate great food and drank fine wine as we put this book together. I promised to include Dario's address—3075 Slocan St., Vancouver, B.C.—and his phone number—(604) 430-2195 —so that you too may call ahead and reserve a lunch of your own.

Peter Legge
Vancouver, B.C.

CONTENTS

Foreword

1. Mr. Legge — You're Fired 19
2. It Began At Chartwell 27
3. Read, Read, Read 37
4. The Little Engine That Did 45
5. A Package Of Dynamite 51
6. Dare to Be An Eagle 59
7. A Real Treasure 67
8. O Canada 73
9. Fathers 83
10. Attitude Is Everything 99
11. Dosen 107
12. The Rocket 113
13. A Dozen Quickies 123
14. Dare To Be Fat Free 131
15. The Astronaut 137
16. From Russia With 50 Ruples 141
17. The "Real" Great One 153
18. Fore — Charity 159
19. A Lesson In Leadership 163
20. The Speakers Roundtable 177
21. Fear vs. Courage: It's Your Choice 181
22. The Three Steps To Building
    A Winner's Attitude 185
23. You Can Live An Amazing Life 205

FOREWORD

HATCHARD'S PICCADILLY IN LONDON describes itself as the most beautiful book shop in the world, and until another comes along to claim the title, I will agree. Hatchard's is indeed beautiful, and as bountiful as you would ever want a book shop to be, the kind of emporium that stirs the senses with its lore and its unbelievable London loveliness.

Among its other many attributes, Hatchard's has two Royal Seals—not the kind that bark—to let us all know that they supply books not only to Charles, the Prince of Wales, but also to Philip, the Duke of Edinburgh. The Queen isn't mentioned. I must presume that she's a fan of dot.com.

Anyway, on one of my trips to London, I ended up as I often do, at Hatchard's. If not to buy, then certainly to browse. London, among many other things, is an awfully good browsing town.

As November rains swept the statuary of Piccadilly, I navigated the stacks and tables of Hatchard's, but couldn't find the book I was looking for, "The Complete Encyclopedia of the SAS" by Barry Davies, British Empire Medal.

Having shared this disappointment with my dinner companions, one of my Variety International board members, Neil Sinclair and his wife Pamela, I thought nothing more about it until late the next afternoon when wrapped in a distinguished Hatchard's bag, with a note from Pamela and Neil, came the elusive book.

Like just about everyone, I know very little about Britain's Special Air Service, because since it first came into being, that's the way the SAS has wanted it. Eminently effective as a force against foul deeds of many kinds, and very, very secret. I also figured that if this book was any good at all, I could add to my knowledge on the long flight back home to Canada. Published by Virgin, and of coffee table dimension, it cost 25 British pounds.

If I may quote from the inside flap, you will get an inkling of what the SAS is all about. From A to Z, there is, of course, much more inside.

"Since its origin during World War II to its role today as the world's premier anti-terrorist unit, Britain's Special Air Service has been home to the most highly trained and deadly soldiers ever to do battle. An awesome military machine shrouded in secrecy, the regiment has entered the mythology of the modern military age."

The encyclopedia, written by a man who served with the SAS for 18 years, claims to penetrate the legend to provide "the first definitive reference to every aspect of the history of the British Army's elite fighting force, and its brothers-in-arms [no mention of sisters in arms!] in the Australian, New Zealand and Rhodesian SAS."

While the book, with more than 1,000 cross-referenced entries, may include more information than most of us need, its effect, supported by hundreds of pictures of key people, maps, plans, weaponry and other easy-to-read data, really *is* a chronology of great courage. And a terrific browse on the way home.

As I learned from the entry **Stirling**, the SAS was born of a good idea. In 1940 Lieutenant David Stirling was serving with No. 8 Commando in North Africa.

"In the belief that a small band of dedicated men could operate successfully behind the enemy lines, he managed to present his plan to General Ritchie, who at the time was Deputy Chief of Staff. His idea and memorandum finally reached the Commander-in-Chief of the Middle East, General Auchinleck, and the SAS was born."

David Stirling is quoted as saying, 'We believe, as did the ancient Greeks who originated the word aristocracy, that every man with the right attitude and talents, regardless of birth and riches, has a capacity in his own lifetime of reaching that status in its true sense. In fact, in our SAS context, an individual soldier might prefer to go on serving as an NCO rather than leave the regiment in order to obtain an officer's commission. All ranks in the SAS are of "one company" in which a sense of class is both alien and ludicrous.'

Lieutenant Stirling was captured in North Africa and sent to an Italian prison at Gavi, where he escaped "at least four times." Transferred to the notorious German fortress at Colditz, he was a prisoner there until the end of the war. Stirling was knighted in 1990 for his services. He died the same year.

There are few modern theatres of conflict where the SAS has not been involved. Gulf War? They were there. Iranian Embassy in London? There. So too the Falklands, Northern Ireland, Vietnam, Borneo, Rhodesia, Oman, and many more. And always, an intriguing tale of grassroots involvement, deadly force when needed, and, depending on the assignment and the territory, unique and creative understanding.

All of this is really a preamble to what I remember as the encyclopedia's main message, and what really triggered the inspiration for this book and its title.

At the beginning of each letter section in the encyclopedia is a rendering of the SAS emblem and its incorporated motto, which Mr. Davies says was allegedly formulated by Lieutenant Stirling. The emblem is a winged dagger, the legendary Excalibur of King Arthur. Shades of blue on the emblem represent the colors of Oxford and Cambridge.

And the motto that I found so meaningful? Who Dares Wins!

What simple, powerful words, and what a strong, strong message. It has seen the SAS through 60 years of courageous history, and when I thought about it, a message that has propelled much of my own life, that I have observed and admired many times in others.

This book is about people who dared, and who won—becoming true aristocrats of our always-surprising human race.

May their life victories inspire your own.

Peter Legge
Vancouver, B.C.
April, 2001

CHAPTER 1

Mr. Legge — You're Fired

IN THE SUMMER OF 1976 I was general sales manager of a radio station in British Columbia's Fraser Valley, just east of Vancouver. On a Thursday morning just before noon—we remember these days and times—the station's president fired me.

A short memo to the staff said: "Peter Legge is no longer employed by this station. It will be business as usual." The note was signed "The President."

Business as usual? Maybe for the station, but certainly not for me.

I'm not the first or last person ever to be fired. But for me it *was* the first time, and I pledged right then that it would be the last.

As with anyone who has ever been fired, I wondered why it had happened. I thought I'd done a pretty good job handling the sales department, competing with the bigger Vancouver radio market, exceeding sales budgets every month and getting the station recognized far beyond our broadcast borders. For three years we had even scooped up the World Hockey Association broadcast rights, and sold them out. I thought things were going pretty well. I'd even made a costly personal investment in the station.

There is no question that the owner and I had philosophical differences, and while I resented and strongly disagreed with his reasons for my termination, it *was* his station, and he had every right to decide who would work for him and who would not. Clearly I didn't fit into his plans and was let go.

But you know what? Sometimes, actually *often,* a cataclysmic thing like being fired can change your life. It certainly changed mine.

My departure from that station was the catalyst for actions that set me on a course of daring and courageous decisions—some of the biggest I had ever made. Courageous? I was heavily in debt, my house was mortgaged to the hilt, and I had cashed in all my life insurance to buy 10 per cent of the station. And now I was out on the street. No severance pay, no termination pay, nothing.

Things were tough. For a while my parents even dropped off hampers of food so my wife and I and our very young daughter could eat. I was down about as far as I could go. But I was not out!

I was watching *Gone with the Wind* one night when something hit me. Halfway through the movie, Scarlett was whipping her poor horse as it pulled her cart along the road back to Tara. Hungry and exhausted, the horse died.

Scarlett got out of her buggy, fell to her knees, picked up some earth and said: "As God is my witness, I will never go hungry again."

In my own despair, I heard her message loud and clear. The scene and Scarlett's words struck a chord in my heart and I have repeated them to myself for 25 years.

I knew right then that I had to be fully responsible for the condition I now found myself in; it was I who had to be the architect of my own future. I could no longer blame the world, the station president, or any other "philosophical differences" real or imagined for what had happened. I had to get my life together, dream a better dream, take complete responsibility for all of my actions. I had to get up from the sorry state I was in, and move forward.

I had to dare big time. But this time I would win.

I heard about a little magazine called *TV Week* that had

gone into bankruptcy. Its printer, The Columbian Co., had inherited the publication when its printing bill went unpaid. While The Columbian had an interest in printing *TV Week*, the company was not interested in becoming its publisher. They needed a publisher.

When you're down, you need to be bold. I heard about the opportunity, and coming from the media business, and still considering myself to be a pretty good salesman, I approached the new owners to make a potential deal. I ended up buying 50 per cent of the magazine for the unpaid printing bill of $76,000. I would pay the bill out of subsequent profits.

My first day as publisher was April 3, 1976. In a rented back room of a Vancouver print shop, with a staff of just three, we went to work, assembling listings, selling advertising, developing editorial material, and seeking a network to circulate the 'we try harder' TV listings for a market that didn't really need us. When you have *TV Guide,* who needs *TV Week*?

As we now say in our corporate brochure and on our web site, no one suspected that this humble foray into Canadian publishing would put us on a fast track to success. We sold *TV Week* for 10 cents a copy, and in the first year our sales topped $70,000. *TV Week* took on a giant, and with panache, style and enthusiasm, we began to beat him at his own game. We were local, we were different, and we were better. Our initial success spurred new ventures. We began to gather the beginnings of a great army of enthusiasts who would nurture Canada Wide Magazines into maturity, to make it the publishing force that it is today.

Our acquisitions and product development over the last 25 years have established Canada Wide as the largest independent publisher in Western Canada. Our $25-million company now employs more than 100 professionals in our Burnaby, B.C. headquarters and we have sales offices in Calgary and Toronto.

TV Week has become British Columbia's premier TV listings magazine and the second-largest-selling magazine in the province. From our beginning with *TV Week*, we now publish 20 major titles, including business, consumer, leisure and trade magazines—that rattle out at a rate of more than 17 million copies a year. And we have diversified. Our dynamic growth has allowed Canada Wide to expand its talents to include graphic design, direct marketing and fundraising.

Has everything we have done been entirely successful? No, it hasn't. But that's what any business is all about—being able to revel in the glory times and sweat the difficulties, learn from mistakes and bad decisions.

I hope that those who serve Canada Wide—and what a remarkable family it has been—will agree that we share our triumphs and tragedies, that despite any hiccups along the way, our optimism for tomorrow always remains high.

Canada Wide has established itself as a publishing powerhouse by drawing upon the business savvy of its people, a high work ethic, and universal commitment to quality. I would like to share the core values that collectively make up our mission to be Western Canada's dynamic leader in the magazine publishing industry.

The first is **Honesty**. Honesty and integrity in all of our business dealings, both inside Canada Wide and outside the company, are cornerstones of our business.

The second is **Competency**. We are committed to encouraging, developing and maintaining the highest levels of professional expertise in every employee to ensure excellence in all aspects of the products and services we provide.

The third is **Vision**. We are committed to keeping our eyes trained on the future and to encourage the sharing of new ideas among all of our employees.

The fourth is **Profitability**. We are committed to thoughtful planning and responsive management in all sectors of the company to ensure the company's ongoing financial success.

The fifth is **Customer Service**. We are committed to developing a thorough understanding of the unique needs of every client and to developing and delivering top-quality products that fully meet those needs.

The sixth is **Meaningful Employment with a Future**. We are committed to the growth and development of all of our employees and to ensuring their success and future within Canada Wide.

The seventh is **Community Involvement**. We are committed to supporting charitable endeavors and to putting our resources to work for the betterment of the community.

Integral to all of these values, we believe that success is the pursuit of a worthy ideal.

In the rush of things, core values that we develop for our companies and ourselves sometimes end up on the back burner. While we sometimes err, we try to keep them up front. They are integral to the dynamics of a living, breathing organization.

Every July, *BCBusiness*, one of our premier publications, recognizes British Columbia's top 100 companies. This annual scorecard attracts tons of attention, and we capitalize on the always-exciting results by hosting a big downtown lunch that attracts more than a thousand business fans. In 2000, our guest speaker at the luncheon was Rubin "Hurricane" Carter, who you will recall spent 20 years behind bars for murders he didn't commit. The Denzel Washington film on Hurricane's incredible life was a huge success, and it set the real Hurricane off on a whole new career of powerful public speaking.

As a speaker for our *BCBusiness* luncheon, Hurricane was a delight.

"When a black man escapes the electric chair," he said in his introduction, "it's not just a pleasure to be *here*, it's a pleasure to be *anywhere!*"

A big fan of the kind of messages that Hurricane delivers, I took some notes during his presentation and they are worth sharing.

During his incarceration, Hurricane Carter often ended up in solitary, the prison's infamous 'hole.'

"The hole makes it possible for me to see reality," he said. "Because you can't look out, you *have* to look in." I thought back to the beginnings of my own publishing career, and the still, small voice that drove me in new directions.

"In the dark, I couldn't see the color of my skin. I became part of the human race."

The man's messages are full of optimism—as are those of so many people who have experienced great difficulty, who have suffered and won.

"Today is what it is because yesterday is what it was," he said. "Tomorrow will be exactly what we make of today."

The message I got from Hurricane Carter is that we have an obligation to seize opportunity, and even if the rules change—as they certainly did for him, and long ago, for me—even if the ladder of success is sometimes up against the wrong wall, obstacles make us stronger. Lost dreams need not be lost forever.

Dare to dream, he said. And by daring, win.

We have done that.

My thanks to everyone who has played a part in Canada Wide's continuing success. I owe you all a debt of gratitude.

CHAPTER 2

It Began At Chartwell

VANCOUVER'S JOE SEGAL is the kind of guy who, no matter what he's doing, demonstrates that humankind has the potential to be nothing short of remarkable. Every community should have a Joe Segal, because we need people like him to give the rest of us hope that there *is* hope.

I've known Joe for many years, and look to him as a great mentor in business and in life. A confessed groupie, I have, like many other individuals and businesses, been the recipient of his wise counsel. A lunch at the Four Seasons' Chartwell Restaurant with Joe goes beyond the best of food.

Because you may be reading this in a location that is far removed from my own habitat of Vancouver, British Columbia, let me tell you something of Joe's background, and why I have included him and his wife Rosalie in this book about daring and winning. Much of this is a steal from his official biography.

Joseph Segal—I have never called him Joseph!—was born in Vegreville, Alberta, famous not only for Joe, but for a giant decorated Easter egg that respects the community's Ukrainian heritage. Joe moved to Edmonton at the age of 12, at 17 worked on the Alaska highway, and soon after that joined the Calgary Highlanders, for whom he served overseas for two years during the Second World War.

On his discharge from the army in 1946, he came to Vancouver, met Rosalie Wosk, and decided to stay. Two years later they were married.

After a short stint in real estate, Joe started selling war surplus merchandise. In 1950, he opened his first Field's store, and by 1976, he owned 85 stores and had acquired Zeller's. Three years later, Zeller's merged with the Hudson's Bay Company, and Joe continued to take over and successfully develop many other companies. In 1989, during his chairmanship of the Simon Fraser University Development Committee, Joe spearheaded the establishment of the university's downtown campus. He is Chancellor Emeritus of Vancouver's Simon Fraser University and has served on its Board of Governors for 18 years. He is a life governor of the Louis Brier Home for the Aged, a Board member of the Vancouver Police Foundation, of Pearson College, of the Matinée Ltd. Fashion Foundation, of the Schara Tzedeck Cemetery Board, and of the Jewish Federation of Greater Vancouver. He is an honorary member of the BC Society of Landscape Architects, an Honorary Trustee of Yeshiva University of New York and an honorary supporter of Volunteer Vancouver.

There's more. Joe has served on the Board of B.C.'s Children's Hospital Foundation, the Bank of Canada, the Vancouver Aquarium and the Council for Canadian Unity. He has been a director-at-large for the National Board of Junior Achievement of Canada and was Chairman of Special Gifts for the Canadian National Institute for the Blind Capital Campaign. In 1971, he was named the first Man of the Year for State of Israel Bonds.

For his services, Joe has earned many awards. He is a member of both the Order of Canada and the Order of British Columbia. He is the recipient of an Honorary Doctor of Laws Degree from Simon Fraser University and of the university's Distinguished Leadership Award. In 1988, he was named Vancouver Entrepreneur of the Year. Joe and Rosalie were honored with United Way's Award of Distinction for their outstanding contributions to

United Way and the community. Joe has received the Philanthropic Leadership Award from the Association of Fundraising Professionals of BC, the Variety Club Golden Heart Award, the Vancouver Junior Board of Trade Award of Excellence as 1999 Community Service Leader of the Year, the Downtown Business Improvement Award, the BC Apparel Industry Lifetime Achievement Award and the Distinguished Service Award from the Union of Jewish Congregations of America for dedication to service to youth. The year 2000 brought a new honor to Joe when his name was included in the list of the top 100 people who have shaped the province of British Columbia in the past century. Joe's most recent honor was the Freedom of the City Medal presented to him by Vancouver Mayor Philip Owen.

But all of that—and only Joe knows what drives his endless good works—still doesn't make the picture of this dapper, silver-haired, always unassuming man complete. Not just an entrepreneur and a philanthropist, he is also a man who loves his wife, his family, and the extended family in his community.

When, in the spring of 2000, I was asked to be master of ceremonies for a dinner that would honor Joe and Rosalie for their work for State of Israel Bonds, I said it would be a great honor. The only challenge, of course, would be in deciding how my remarks might reflect the awe I had for this man and his equally amazing wife.

As I sometimes do—and it seemed to be fitting for this event—I went to the Bible for inspiration, and found it in the Old Testament.

I told the audience how my wife and I had made a recent trip to Israel, and how, during our visit, we had ended up one day in the Valley of Elah, west of Bethlehem, and the supposed site of one of the Bible's great stories of courage and entrepreneurship, even if 3,000 years ago entrepreneurship might have gone by a different name!

As the story goes, and I'll try to get it right, there was a standoff in the valley between two long-standing enemies, the Israelites and the Philistines. Heading up the Israelites, King Saul was tall and handsome, but not made of the stuff of battle. The nominee of the Philistines was Goliath, a nine-foot WWF-like giant, who was ready for anything.

In King Saul's place, a teenager named David volunteered to fight the giant Goliath, and the obliging king offered his huge armor, helmet and sword as defence. But nothing fit. It was a case of right outfit, wrong person. Appropriate for Saul, inappropriate for David.

Like any teenager, David liked to travel light, and instead of trying to wrestle himself into armor, he chose a different kind of weaponry, five smooth stones from a convenient stream. Propelling these state-of-the-art missiles with a hand-held sling, he conked the great Goliath, then decapitated the giant. The Philistines fled and David won the day for the Israelites.

I told my audience that David found his comfort zone. Not the unfamiliar ill-fitting armor of another, but a weapon he knew well—a simple sling and a handful of stones.

When I was in the Valley of Elah, I thought about that far-off, triumphant day when David slew Goliath, and I picked up five smooth stones from a brook and brought them back to Canada. For me, they are wonderful icons about daring and winning—and when I spoke at Joe's dinner, I took them along to make some additional points.

I suggested that when young Joe Segal arrived in Vancouver after the war, he too came with five metaphorical smooth stones that were to shape his life.

Stone No. 1, I said, was family. For Joe and Rosalie, family comes first—what they give in so many ways to each other, their four children and their 11 grandchildren.

Stone No. 2 was all about character, and I read this piece about reputation and character:

The circumstances amid which you live determine your reputation;
The truth you believe determines your character.

Reputation is what you are supposed to be;
Character is what you are.

Reputation is the photograph;
Character is the face.

Reputation comes over one from without;
Character grows up from within.

Reputation is what you have when you come to a new
community;
Character is what you have when you go away.

Your reputation is made in a moment;
Your character is built in a lifetime.

Your reputation is learned in an hour;
Your character does not come to light for a year.

Reputation grows like a mushroom;
Character lasts like eternity.

Reputation makes you rich or makes you poor;
Character makes you happy or makes you miserable.

Reputation is what men say about you on your tombstone;
Character is what the angels say about you before the
throne of God.

Stone No. 3 was about having a sense of humor. And when David was going to take on this giant of a Goliath, some people said: "He's so big, you can't beat him." And David replied: "He's so big, I can't miss!"

When Joe Segal left tiny Vegreville for big-city Vancouver, his friends said: "It's so big, you can't succeed." And Joe said: "It's so big, I can't miss!"

For 35 years, Field's—Joe's stores—promised in their radio spots that their pyjamas were shrink resistant. They shrink, said the spots, but they don't really want to!

Stone No. 4, I said, was about leadership. In all of his endeavors, from the United Way to Simon Fraser University, from life as a retailer, to life as a worker for his faith, Joe stamped everything with his own brand of leadership.

Vancouver, I said, was not built by men and women who relied on others to take care of them. It was built by people who relied on themselves, who dared to shape their own lives, who had enough courage to blaze new trails, enough confidence in themselves to take the necessary risks. That, I said, was Joe.

I said that cities, provinces, states and countries need inspirational leadership, and so do businesses and families. We need more Joe Segals.

I said that the last word most of us would associate with leadership would be *loneliness*. But my experience is that the best leaders are lonely because they are thinkers. In his book "Leadership Jazz," Max DePree says that there are no short-cuts to preparing for leadership. Polishing one's gifts, he says, requires the tumbling of experiences and the grit of great discipline. Preparation comes not from books. Real preparation consists of hard work and wandering in the desert, much feedback, much forgiveness and years of failure.

If you are a leader, people will want to follow. But it's lonely out front. Leadership calls for personal security, ethical integrity, and moral purity. All three must be cultivated in private, where it's lonely. I told the guests at Joe's dinner that he had all of these qualities.

Joe once told me that one of life's problems is not that we aim too high and fail. It's that we aim too low and succeed.

And Stone No. 5 I saved for Rosalie, Joe's wife of 50 years. Rosalie has supported all of his endeavors, his business and community activities. Who knows how many millions she has helped raise at dinners she has hosted in the Segal home? From Red Cross to St. John Ambulance and United Way, the list is endless, and the benefits to these and other organizations have been tremendous.

But it is not always up front and glamorous. I heard a story that during one holiday season Rosalie phoned daughters Tracy and Sandra to announce that they would be serving dinners to the homeless of East Vancouver at the

Salvation Army. She was on her way to pick them up.

Rosalie's acts of humanity are away from the limelight of public recognition. She is indeed a wife of noble character.

The stones I brought home from the Valley of Elah, like those picked up and flung by slim David, have served me well, and will continue to do so.

They remind me that you can't go into battle in the armor of another. You have to go in with talents of your own. Risky? You bet. But remember, when they're big, you can't miss them—and the bigger they are, the harder they fall.

As Joe would say: Set your sights high, and win the day.

CHAPTER 3

Read, Read, Read

THOSE WHO DARE TO READ, WIN.

I've heard it said that the book you haven't read won't help you. I agree. And how about this? If it's a crime to be unable to read—and in this allegedly enlightened age, it surely is—then it's a far worse crime to be able to read and to never pick up a book.

Research has shown that many university students never

crack open a hardcover book after they graduate. Ninety per cent of the population hardly read at all. Ten per cent read a book a year on a topic of personal interest, or one that has something to do with a vocation. Interesting statistics.

The first business book I ever read was written by one of North America's most successful insurance salesmen—a gentleman called Elmer G. Leterman. Harper and Row first published his book "How Showmanship Sells" in 1965, when, I should note, the price tag was a mere $3.95. It was the fourth book by Mr. Leterman. The other three were "The New Art of Selling," "Personal Power Through Creative Selling," and "The Sale Begins When the Customer Says No." Elmer Leterman, who through his written messages became a personal mentor, was dubbed one of America's 12 master salesmen.

I doubt if any of Leterman's books are available today, but I still have "How Showmanship Sells." As a young radio salesman, this motivational book was an invaluable tool. Not only did its messages provide me with sound knowledge that would pump my career, but also it was a catalyst for more reading, more learning from others. After Leterman came motivators like Brian Tracy, Og Mandino, Harvey Mackay, Denis Waitley and others—and I've read them all.

In his writing Elmer Leterman reinforced an old and good message—one of the great secrets of success is that you can acquire it by sticking close to and learning from successful people.

Forty years later, one of my professional speaking mentors, Nido R. Qubein, said that his parents told him: "If you are looking for success, walk hand in hand with men and women who are more successful than you are." The same strong message.

Author and international speaker Brian Tracy has spent the last 25 years studying what he calls the laws of success. He asked the question: "Why do some people succeed and some don't?" Tracy discovered that there was a consistent and predictable pattern of similarities that seemed to accompany all business success. One of those patterns was a commitment to reading, the study of other successful people, and the application of their successful attributes.

Abraham Lincoln said: "I shall study and prepare myself, and someday my chance will come." And it surely did. In Brian Tracy's latest work "The 100 Absolutely Unbreakable Laws of Business Success" he says, "success is not an accident. Success is the definite result of continuous, persistent action in the unrelenting pursuit of your goals in a manner consistent with universal laws."

One of those laws is studying and reading about success, and applying these ideas to your own life. Try it. Open a book and learn from those whom you admire, from those whom you have judged to be successful. And follow through. Dare to read, and win!

In Leterman's first book, the messages of which work as well today as they did when I first read it, is this "letter-gram," which is full of sound, practical advice:

The largest room in the world
Is the room for improvement.

It's not the hours you put in,
It's what you put in the hours.

You will never find time for anything,
If you want time, you must make it.

Short visits make long friendships.

Everyone is able to give pleasure in some way,
One may do it by coming into a room, another by going out.

There is no use itching about something unless
You are willing to scratch for it.

The person who never does more than he gets paid for
Never gets paid for any more than he does.

There are better ways of stopping your mouth,
Than by putting your foot in it.

Say what you can back up,
And then back up what you say.

The dictionary is the only place where
Success comes before work.

I don't intend to grow old gracefully,
I'm fighting every step of the way.

Charlie "Tremendous" Jones, another great author and motivational speaker, said that we will be the same as we are today in five years except for the people we have met, the places we have been, and the books we have read. Since Elmer's first book encounter, I've made time to not only read hundreds of books but to author five of my own, including this one—because I believe that success secrets should be shared.

Here, at no extra charge, is a Legge list of 50 favorite books you may wish to include in your library. Dare to read a book a week, and one of the universal laws that nourishes success will transform your life.

The Bible – without question the single most important book ever. Period. The inspired word of God to shape every aspect of your life. Indispensable to the building of your library.

The Power of Positive Thinking – Dr. Norman Vincent Peale

Think and Grow Rich – Napoleon Hill

How to Win Friends and Influence People – Dale Carnegie

As A Man Thinketh – James Allen

See You at the Top – Zig Ziglar

Swim with the Sharks – Harvey Mackay

Focus or Failure – James H. Amos, Jr.

The Road Less Travelled – M. Scott Peck

The Greatest Salesman in the World – Og Mandino

Live Your Dreams – Les Brown

Developing The Leader Within You – John C. Maxwell

Timing is Everything – Denis Waitley

7 Habits of Highly Effective People – Stephen Covey

Maximum Achievement – Brian Tracy

Boom, Bust & Echo – David K. Foot

What Makes The Great Great – Dennis Kimbro, PhD

The New Dynamics of Winning – Denis Waitley

You Can Have It All – Mary Kay

The Power of Optimism – Alan Loy McGinnis

Stairway to Success – Nido Qubein

Go For the Magic – Pat Williams

The Winner Within – Pat Riley

Attitude is Everything – Keith D. Harrell

Jesus CEO – Laurie Beth Jones

Seven Miracles of Management – Alan Downs

It's Easier to Succeed Than Fail – S. Truett Cathy

Life is Tremendous – Charlie "T" Jones

The Millionaire's Mind – Dr. Stanley

Patton on Leadership – Alan Axelrod

The Acorn Principle – Jim Cathcart

How High Can You Bounce? – Roger Crawford

The Magic of Thinking Big – David J. Schwartz, PhD

Elizabeth I CEO – Alan Axelrod

The Biology of Success – John Arnott

*The 100 Absolutely Unbreakable Laws of
    Business Success* – Brian Tracy

Leadership by the Book – Ken Blanchard

Customers For Life – Carl Sewell

The Wealth & Poverty of Nations – David S. Landes

Empires of the Mind – Denis Waitley

The Seasons of Life – Jim Rohn

Million Dollar Habits – Robert J. Ringer

What They Don't Teach You At Harvard Business School –
    Mark H. McCormack

Never Give In – Stephen Mansfield

Making A Difference – Sheila Murray Bethel

Half Time – Bob Buford

The Case For Christ – Lee Strobel

Built to Last – James C. Collins

The Packer Way – Ron Wolf

The Secret of Success – R.C. Allen

CHAPTER 4

The Little Engine That Did

WE ALL HAVE good ideas from time to time. Some of them are brilliant ideas—ideas that if effectively executed may well change the world. I know that I've had lots of them, and I would guess that you have too. When it comes to having good ideas, we are all equally creative.

The problem is that somewhere between the formation of a good idea, the moment that the light bulb goes on, and the potential execution of that good idea, things sometimes go wrong. We lose our enthusiasm because execution seems like too much work. Doubts creep in. We don't want to sweat the research. We lose confidence because we begin to fear that the end result may prove in one way or another that the idea really wasn't that good in the first place.

And then we discover that someone else not only had the same good idea, but they went all the way with it! And we're doubly upset.

Don't let good ideas die. If you believe they have merit, run with them. All the way. Which leads me to a story about a train that began as nothing more than a good idea. But first, as they say on the talk shows, I have to set it up.

Grace McCarthy is a lady well known in my home Canadian province of British Columbia. A businesswoman, former provincial politician, and doer of infinite good deeds, Grace, more than anything else, is a woman who executes her good ideas. Others became involved along the way, but it was Grace who made it official that British Columbia is Beautiful, a label that has been proudly with us for years. It was Grace who was the force behind EXPO 86, a remarkable world fair that changed the shape of downtown Vancouver, and repositioned the city's attitude about its place in the world community. It was Grace who twisted arms to light the graceful arches of Vancouver's Lions Gate Bridge to make it an even more spectacular icon at the entrance to the city's harbor. It was Grace who in recent times founded a program that would raise millions to help fight deadly bowel diseases in children. Grace makes grand and wonderful things happen.

In 1994, Grace McCarthy, who is a former British Columbia Minister of Tourism, had a brilliant idea to help pump business in Vancouver. What she figured was that when it comes to making tourists to the city feel welcome, no one should be able to do it better than the uniformed doormen at every hotel in the city. After the cab drivers, they are the first ambassadors of welcome for visitors, and if they do it right, they have the ability to set the tone for endless guest visits to their city.

Executing a good idea, Grace sponsored the world's first international doormen's convention, and in typical style, pulled it off with great flair. Delegate doormen came from as far away as Raffles in Singapore, from Hong Kong, Bangkok, New York, Hawaii, Los Angeles, Las Vegas—and of course from all of the major hotels in Vancouver, and British Columbia's capital city, Victoria.

Grace asked me to be a keynote speaker for the convention, and being a frequent traveller, hotel user and city booster, I was delighted to accept. In lieu of payment, they made me an honorary doorman. What that meant, apart from being welcomed into a great international fraternity, was that whenever I have speaking assignments at hotels in Vancouver, they pick up the parking tab. And with the cost of parking these days, it was a fabulous gesture!

OK, it's a long introduction, but that's the setup, and it segues into a story about a doorman who dared.

When Peter Armstrong was a doorman at the Hotel Vancouver, he talked with colleague Murray Atherton one day about how he felt about the organized tours on which he was obliged as a doorman to send the hotel's guests. Murray remembers him saying that the whole process was really a bind. Guests had to take taxis to bus terminals, stand in queues, hunt for departure gates, and suffer frustrations that shouldn't be part of a relaxing holiday. There had to be another way.

"Peter had a vision for a travel business that would provide one-stop service and individualized attention—and he was determined to fill that need," said Murray. And by golly, he did. Like Grace McCarthy, who was a catalyst for change, and who made her good ideas happen in events like the doormen's convention, Peter Armstrong made his good idea happen. Today he is president and CEO of the Great Canadian Railtour Company, the owner and operator of Rocky Mountaineer Railtours.

Rocky Mountaineer, and you may have already heard of it, or even better, have taken a trip on it, offers a combination of spectacular scenery and romantic daytime train travel to people eager to retrace the legendary Western Canadian routes of North America's first transcontinental railway. Travelling between Vancouver and the Rocky Mountains, it is the largest privately owned passenger rail operator in North America, with more than 350 employees and sales representation in 18 countries. Great Canadian has a fleet of more than 60 pieces of rolling stock, including eight custom-designed two-level dome coaches, built at a cost of $2.8 million apiece. Rocky Mountaineer's schedule expanded in 2000 to include a total of 148 departures between mid-April and mid-October. Its luxurious cars are packed with no-flap vacationers from around the world— just as Peter dreamed would someday happen.

Senior vice-president and chief operating officer James Terry says that Rocky Mountaineer has grown consistently since it began.

"Every year, we've expanded service, and every year we've run very high occupancy," he says. "Rail travel has seen a great resurgence. It's a leisurely way for people young and old to explore this part of the country."

Great Canadian won its right to serve in March 1990, and Peter Armstrong lost no time bringing in a host of former railway executives and tourism experts who offered a collective 120 years of knowledge to his new venture. Terry says that from day one the company operated as a tourism firm with the central product being the train. Before long, passengers were clambering aboard at a rate of 600 per trip, and in short order *International Railway Traveller* magazine voted Rocky Mountaineer "one of the twenty best rail experiences in the world." New prospects were hitting the company's virtual-tour web site www.rockymountaineer.com

more than a thousand times a day.

Service on board the train is provided at the highest possible level. The Onboard Attendants have been specially trained to provide individual service—remember the need and the good idea?—and a running commentary on what's outside. Pre-season educational sessions presided over by botanists, geologists and historians are responsible for the impressive knowledge that the train staff shares with guests.

Their peers have recognized the efforts of former doorman Armstrong and his team. Early in 2000, Rocky Mountaineer was honored with the Best Tourism Marketing Campaign award at the first annual British Columbia Tourism Awards. The firm also received honorable mention for the Environmentally Responsible Tourism award sponsored by the Oceans Blue Foundation. New routes and schedules were added in 2000, bringing even more of Grace McCarthy's Beautiful British Columbia closer to many more people.

Former doorman Murray Atherton, now vice president of marketing and sales for the company, says: "The most exciting thing about Rocky Mountaineer Railtours is not the markets we are in, but the ones that are yet to come."

Dream big dreams. Get an idea. Make it happen!

CHAPTER 5

A Package of Dynamite

THERE ARE PEOPLE in this book you won't know, and most likely never will. I have chosen to include their names and to tell their stories because I figured that if these people inspired me, you too may wish to read about them, and learn something about their lives and their successes.

Wendy P. Lisogar-Cocchia of Vancouver is a diminutive bundle of pure dynamite, and among the many honors she has received for her work for business and some very special personal charities, I add my own. Wendy P. Lisogar-Cocchia has Dared and Won.

Wendy's day job is to serve as executive vice president of Vancouver's 250 all-suite Century Plaza Hotel & Spa Group, and as president of Spa at the Century, a spectacular centre of health and relaxation that in 1997 revitalized the hotel's lobby and made a proud name for itself in about two minutes flat. As part of the family business, Wendy also operates another hotel and three rental and commercial apartment complexes in and around Greater Vancouver.

Just 36 years of age at this writing, Wendy has been honored, among other things, as a YWCA Woman of Distinction, as a Vancouver Sales and Marketing Executive of the Year, as one of Business in Vancouver's 40 under 40 honorees, as Variety Club International corporate fundraiser of distinction, and as a Canadian Travel Person of the Year.

It would take more than a chapter in this book to discover exactly what makes Wendy run, but run she does—and always gives the appearance that tomorrow for her will be even bigger and better, that her race has really only just begun.

I've seen a few hotels along the way, but Wendy, I know, is infused with the love of the hotel game. When you and I were out doing what other 13-year-old kids were doing, Wendy Lisogar was bussing tables in her father's Century Plaza Hotel coffee shop. And making the hotel's beds, vacuuming the hallways, and greeting guests at the front desk. Eight years later, she was running the place.

After graduating from the University of B.C., it had been Wendy's plan to be a student in Cornell University's hotel management program. But soon after graduating from UBC, her father Roy Lisogar suffered a stroke, and Wendy immediately assumed much more business responsibility.

From what was initially a public relations role, she moved on into staff management, taking care of day-to-day operations, signing the cheques, and dreaming new dreams for the well-located downtown property. Under her leadership, business boomed, and for very good reason the Century Plaza became a destination of choice for travellers of every kind. She developed programs that would generate a shift in her traditional client base, and made the hotel a destination for tours from Europe, and groups from the entertainment industry. Her registry showed that recent guests included the stars and casts of *Jesus Christ Superstar, Ice Capades, Stars on Ice, Disney on Ice, Riverdance* and *Forever Tango*. She has implemented new employee incentive programs for her 235 employees, and has initiated a $1-million program of renovation.

Part of this young lady's dream was to build a spa for the hotel. Not just your average couple of rooms with weights, a tub and a treadmill, but a large and luxurious spa that would mean gutting floors, knocking down walls, and turning yesterday's architecture into a space of contemporary luxury.

Founded in 1997, the Spa at the Century was an immediate hit, and in short order was rated the city's best. British Columbia's film industry attracts the biggest, and visiting stars need a place to relax. Among others, Wendy's spa has welcomed Sharon Stone, Gwyneth Paltrow, Gillian Anderson, Uma Thurman, Ethan Hawke and Jeremy Piven. Now bigger and better, the spa has 100 full- and part-time employees. From its initial 372 square metres, the spa went to 743 square metres, then to 1,486. As well as targeting the movie crowd, Wendy's spa found favor with businesspeople of both sexes. Thirty per cent of her customers are men. She also caters to people who have been referred to her program from St. Paul's Hospital right next door.

When Wendy won Marketing Executive of the Year in 1999, Gary Bombay, the club's president, called her innovative and courageous.

She closed a successful bar in the hotel to expand her spa, he said. It takes courage to take a business that is viable and very successful, close it and begin something completely new.

Describing what Wendy had done, local television anchor Jennifer Mather said: "What I find especially innovative is how Wendy created a five-star spa in what essentially is a three-star location. The minute you step through the spa doors, not only are you transported to a luxurious world, but you are treated like a first-class customer.

"What I most admire about Wendy though isn't something you can find in a jar. Her willingness to take risks and try something new, while those around her say it can't be done, is legendary. Her work ethic is second to none, and her personal hands-on approach makes it a refreshing change for business owners who can't seem to move from behind a desk."

But if Wendy's day-to-day businesses are a success, her work for charity is completely over the top.

Around the time that Wendy was being called upon to give her all to the development of the family business, she became founder and chair of the Century Plaza Hotel & Spa Ladies Media Golf Classic. Since 1987, the event has raised more than $1.5 million for charities that benefit children. And of that total, $700,000 went to charities supported by Variety Clubs International.

In two years, she and her very supportive media group met a goal of $375,000 to build a new educational centre for abused children, and raised an additional $350,000 for a new teaching facility for the Vancouver Oral Centre for Deaf Children. Other beneficiaries have included the Down Syndrome Research Foundation, the Canadian Cancer Society, Red Cross, St. John Ambulance, and the United Way of Vancouver.

The event in 2000 raised a record-breaking $202,000 for the Down Syndrome Research Foundation and the BC CHILD Foundation, an acronym for Crohns Disease, Colitis and Liver Disorders in Children.

Wendy's underlying motivation for her volunteer work has been expressed in words she put together in the summer of 2000, and which she kindly sent along to me.

"Being a volunteer," she wrote, "is not a statement of what I do but of who I am. Over the years, I have experienced some of the most personally gratifying moments in my life while acting as a volunteer. It is something that never leaves me. It defines who I am, and provides the inspiration to do more and be more."

She said that she began working as a volunteer at the age of 17.

"I soon realized that the greatest form of wealth in my life would be the opportunity to assist others. Over the years, individuals who are truly extraordinary have blessed me. Their positive attitude to life removes personal limitations and boundaries. From each person that I am fortunate enough to help, I am rewarded with a unique perspective and appreciation of life."

Of the beginnings of her golf classic she wrote: "In 1987, I began an endeavor to found and chair a fundraising event that would support various children's charities. The event began when I was denied entry into a corporate hospitality golf classic. Whoever would have thought that in 1987 the old boys' club would still be going! Our event was called the Century Plaza Hotel & Spa Ladies Media Golf Classic. Aimed at uniting female media and community members, the annual golf tournament brings together a dynamic group of ladies who work toward a common goal of helping children . . .

"Each year, I hope to do more and accomplish more. However, the reward does not come from how many children I have helped, but knowing that I have been able to make a difference in at least one child's life and to one family. I encourage everyone to be a volunteer in at least one person's life. Whether it is working on something like our golf classic or with a neighbor's child, we can make a tremendous difference.

"As I look forward to all of the things I hope to accomplish as a volunteer, I think back to the time when I presented a dream to a five-year-old, hearing-impaired child. We were able to send this child and her family to Ireland to visit a grandma for the first time. My feelings as I saw the excitement in that child's eyes were indescribable. Moments like that encourage me, and give focus to my life. Being a volunteer is and will be the best thing I ever do."

As I said, a diminutive package of pure dynamite!

CHAPTER 6

Dare To Be An Eagle

I WAS WATCHING THE NEWS ONE NIGHT in this summer of 2000 and learned with great delight that bald eagles, after a period of goodness knows how long, had returned to the vicinity of Washington, DC. In an election year, every politician in that city of powerful and familiar icons of pure Americana, must have been over the moon with delight. Right there, where it all happens, right above the White House, was the soaring symbol of everything we all believe in!

There's no doubt about it, the eagle, despite scavenging habits that occasionally go on behind the scenes, is a fabulous creature, one that inspires in all of us everything we understand to be the sum of qualities that stir the soul, that lift us to higher, grander plains.

I've had great success with my first book "How to Soar with the Eagles," and I know that the title doesn't hurt one bit in helping to generate sales. After its publication in 1992, eagles became very much part of my life. My office is full of busts, photographs and paintings of eagles, accepted with thanks from appreciative audiences, associates and readers. It's always a delight to come into this aviary and be greeted by images of these wonderful birds that like few others have entered our culture and challenged us to share their vision, to soar with them to new heights of purpose and achievement.

Eagles are among the largest and most powerful birds in the world. Far from the other crowds of feathered fauna, they live in the highest places, in aeries with penthouse views. Eagles teach us commitment. They hunt with purpose, soar above and often through the storms, see beyond the immediate into vistas of opportunity. I've seen them catching salmon in their claws in the coastal waters of British Columbia. It's a hunt to behold. A dive with outstretched talons, a grab, and departure to distant feasting.

For centuries, eagles have been recognized as the Kings

of Birds and the Birds of Kings. Long before the United States chose the eagle over the wild turkey to be incorporated into its lore and imagery, the Romans and others in Europe had settled on the eagle as symbolic of power and authority. The bird is the dominant image in the great seal of the U.S. and the image is a regular icon on the nightly news.

We know about those with eagle eyes, who spot the prizes that others can't see. We know about eagles on the golf course, and treasure the times that they are ours!

I looked up some references in literature.

Shakespeare, always good for an observation, wrote: "A lover's eyes will gaze an eagle blind." Now *there* was a smitten lover!

Gil Atkinson wrote: "You are one of a kind,

Therefore, no one can really predict to what heights you might soar.

Even you will not know until you spread your wings!"

Remember Neil Armstrong's great message on July 20, 1969, from Tranquillity Base on the moon? "The eagle has landed."

"My heart," said Chief Dan George of Vancouver, "soars like an eagle!"

And Isaiah said it well: "They that wait upon the Lord shall renew their strength. They shall mount up with wings of eagles."

We are fortunate in British Columbia to have many, many bald eagles, and the locals know their haunts well. In the winter, they crowd in the hundreds in trees along the riverbanks north of Vancouver to feast on migrating salmon and show us up close just how effective they are in the things they do. Let's review again some of the qualities of an eagle, and why they inspire us:

• They Live at the Highest Levels

Eagles always live at the highest levels. Not in the gutters. Denis Waitley said, "We are all born with the seeds of greatness."

Fledgling eagles are called eaglets—nice name for a publishing company! Eaglets reach a point where they must leave the nest, because no matter how far the drop over the edge, they were born to fly.

The mother coaches them, encourages them, and finally makes the nest so uncomfortable that taking flight is a much better alternative to scat-covered sticks. And soar they do. Remember your first time off the high board? Riding a bike? First interview for a job? Most of us needed a push. But what a great feeling to do it, and succeed.

• Commitment and Attitude

Eagles mate for life. What is success? I believe that desire is the key to motivation, but it is also determination and commitment, an unrelenting pursuit of your goal. Commitment and the right attitude will enable you to attain the success you seek.

• The Storms of Life

Eagles wait for warm currents of air, the thermals that help them to soar, that give lift to their seven-foot wings. When the right wind is beneath their wings, it's easier. When we get into trouble we often flap around, and make mistakes. Wait for the moment, for the rising current of well-timed opportunity. Avoid living life from one crisis to another.

I'm told that the Japanese Twenty-Third Psalm goes something like this: Eagles fly above storms. Never water laden. They rise above storms. Never cower in a branch. Winds of adversity begin to brew. Bring a sense of courage. Grow most in tough times. Great values take you high. Low values do the opposite.

It was Robert Schuller who wrote:

Tough times don't last,

Tough people do.

Rise above the circumstances,

Rise above the storms,

Rise above the adversity,

Don't let tough times control you.

Rise above.

• Vision

An eagle sees its goal and goes for it. Our far-reaching goals need to be written down and visualized if we ever hope to attain them. Eagles have magnificent eyes. They are able to detect the movement they're looking for up to 15 miles away. No creature has better eyes than an eagle. Their eyes are organs of great biological precision.

The Bible says that without vision, we perish. Eagles know that well.

Vision is never limited by circumstance. Vision rises above circumstance. The state of our life, happiness, family, and business is determined by our vision. The brightness of a day, the beauty of a mountain, the sparkle of a river, the lush green of grass, the magnificence of nature.

When he was in his nineties, J.C. Penney said: "My eyesight may be fading but my vision has never been better."

No life ever grows great until it is dedicated, disciplined and focused.

• Eagles Don't Quit

As an eagle gets older it goes through great trauma. Eagles develop problems with their beaks which inhibit their prowess and restrict their hunting skill.

Many of us develop problems with our beaks. It has been said that life and death is in the power of the tongue. We can either lift people up or tear them down. For the eagle, the beak is both a weapon to defend itself, a tool for hunting and for navigation. The beak is a guide for the hunt, and radar to guide it home. Without it, it cannot survive.

What happens is that as the eagle gets older the beak calcifies. They can't hunt, they get lost, and many give up and die. But not all. The strongest take another tack, make another decision. They fly as high as possible to a craggy rock, and with no other eagles around, and in an act that appears almost suicidal, they ram their beak on the rock, again and again, and again and again, until finally the calcium breaks up and falls off. It is an act of spectacular rejuvenation.

The strongest of eagles might well say: "Whatever it takes, I refuse to die, I refuse to give up." The choice has been made to live, fly and hunt again.

We were all born to be eagles, born to fly high. We can make a choice to knock off the calcium of discouragement and get on with it. There will be sacrifices, but the best of observers have all said that there always *will* be sacrifices— and they will make us stronger.

We don't get to choose when we will die. But by golly, we can certainly choose to live right now.

In the middle of the Second World War, Winston Churchill spoke at Harrow in England and said:

"Never give in!

Never give in!

Never, never, never, never!"

And England soared.

Note: This chapter was inspired by a sermon given by my pastor Dr. Gordon MacDonald of Calvary Christian Church in Surrey, B.C.

CHAPTER 7

A Real Treasure

I DIDN'T KEEP AN EXACT TALLY, but in 1999, I'm guessing that
I made close to 100 speeches to a variety of local, national
and international audiences. Sure it meant a ton of flying,
camping in hotel rooms good and bad, and too much time
away from my family. But I enjoyed it, or I wouldn't have
done it.

Reflecting on a year of standing before microphones,

and the ups and downs of all of those presentations, the speech I remember best was the sometimes awkward, right-from-the-heart words that I spoke at the wedding of my daughter Samantha. Make no mistake; speaking at your daughter's wedding is one of fatherhood's greatest challenges, and also an assignment that can stir the greatest pride. If you haven't done it, daring to speak at your daughter's wedding is right up there with just about any risk you may encounter!

As with all of my presentations, I kept the notes from that day, and here, more or less, is what I said:

"On May 18, 1969, the phone rang in our little house in Putney, England, and a voice said: 'It's a girl.'

"I raced to the hospital and there was wife and new mother Kay, all smiles and beaming with pride, with this bundle on her chest.

" 'Isn't she beautiful?' she said. She wasn't, but I said she was!

"And then I realized this was daddy's little girl, my first born. What a responsibility! How unbelievable! What a miracle! I was looking at my very first treasure. The dictionary says this about a treasure: 'Something of great value or worth. A person esteemed as rare or precious. To hold or cherish as precious.'

"My treasure. Matthew 6:21 says: 'For where your treasure is, there will your heart be also.' My children and Kay are the most valuable treasures I have. Kay, Samantha,

Rebecca and Amanda. There also is my heart!"

I went on . . .

"It has been said that we should hold everything in our hands lightly, because it will hurt when God pries our fingers open.

"Today my fingers hurt just a little bit.

"Thirty years ago I held this treasure in my hands, and today they are pried open as another man now holds this treasure. Geoff, welcome to our family. And now it is time to call me Peter, instead of Mr. Legge.

"Let me tell you a little about this fine treasure who is now your wife until death do you part.

"I believe she has learned much from her mother.

She is determined.

She is honorable.

She is loving.

She is a hard worker.

She is a perfectionist.

She has a wonderful sense of humor.

She is highly organized.

She is committed.

She runs a little late at times.

She has great fashion sense.

She is beautiful.

She is kind.

She is thoughtful.

Geoff, she is a treasure!

"So, take care of this very special treasure. Value Sam more than your business success, your wealth, your house, your sports or your friends.

"Treat this treasure with great respect. Nurture this treasure. Cherish this treasure like no other. As I know Sam will cherish you."

And then I said . . .

"She is little only once.

"Grant me the wisdom and patience to teach her to follow God and prepare for what is to come.

"She is little only once.

"Did I take the time to play pretend, to play monster, to read, to cuddle, to tell a story.

"She is little only once.

"Nothing is more important than the school play, summers at Malibu, girl guides, the soccer game, and our holidays in Hawaii . . .

"And then . . . all too soon . . . they grow away, and there is no turning back.

"Allow me memories with no regrets. When I disciplined, did I do it with love? Was I firm? Was I fair? Did I correct and explain with patience?

"And she is growing away. Let me always do my best for her. For the rest of our lives let me be Sam's very best friend.

"I love you, sweetheart!"

CHAPTER 8

O Canada

SHORTLY AFTER THE SECOND WORLD WAR, my father Bernie Legge—you may read more about him in my most recent book "If Only I'd Said That"—decided that post-war England just wouldn't fit into his long-range plans for personal success, for his young and beautiful wife, and for me, his 12-year-old son. Dad decided to move to Canada.

Two things helped him to make this big life decision.

The first was that having had a successful stint in His Majesty's Merchant Marine Navy, during which he served in the Second World War, and circumnavigated the globe nine times, his favorite city in the world was Vancouver. The second reason was that the first ship he sailed in was named *The City of Vancouver,* a 9,000-ton iron-transporting frigate. The signs and the memories had clearly pointed him in the direction of British Columbia.

Dad told me many times that it took "courage and daring" to sell up at "home" in the U.K. and set sail for "unknown" opportunities in Canada, and I never doubted him. Almost 40 years old at the time, he arrived in New Westminster, right next door to Vancouver on British Columbia's Lower Mainland, with just $50 in his pocket. In due course, my mother and I came from England to join him, and at the right time, we all became proud Canadian citizens, and have been blessed with success of all kinds in this very rich country.

A few years ago, I made application to the Canadian government to have an official coat of arms struck for future generations of Legges. The coat of arms was granted to our family on January 14, 1999. And the motto I selected was "with courage and daring." It seemed to reflect a lot about my father, and the rest of us who have battled valiantly in his patriotic footsteps.

My father was proud to be a Canadian citizen, proud of his accomplishments, and proud to wave the Canadian flag.

No matter where or when the Canadian national anthem was played, he stood proudly to attention, marking his great respect for his adopted country. If anyone did otherwise, it invariably distressed him. Others may have chosen to mutter the words or not to sing at all, but my father sang the anthem at the top of his lungs.

On a visit to Ottawa, comedian-philosopher Red Skelton, who was 76 at the time, ended his one-man show with this tribute to Canada, and I shared it with my dad. He was thrilled.

I am a 76-year-old visitor in your country, said Red, and I've always felt that Canada is more than a neighbor is because what we shake across the border is our hands, not our fists.

He went on . . .

The other day I heard your national anthem being sung. Some of the voices were loud, some mumbled the words, and some slipped through it because either they weren't thinking about the meaning of the words, or it had become nothing more than a monotonous song. If I may, I would like to recite your national anthem and give you the meaning that I get from the words.

O Canada

I see mountains and valleys and rivers and trees. It is truly Mother Nature's warehouse.

Our Home and Native Land

Places where families live with dignity on rich soil that shares food and beauty.

True Patriots

Patriotism. A pride, a privilege to say I, me, an individual, a committee of one, dedicate all of my worldly goods to give without self-pity.

In All Thy Sons Command

Powerful youth that gives all of its love and devotion, holding a standard with a maple leaf high in the air. It's a symbol of courage, and wherever it waves there is respect, because your loyalty has given it a dignity that shouts freedom.

With Glowing Hearts We See Thee Rise

A warmth that incubates incentive. Wisdom that sees beyond superstition and ignorance.

The True North

A compass needle that points to inspiring realities.

Strong

Courage beyond that struggle to find a dream and make it come true.

Free

That right for each of us to live his or her own life without fears, threats or any sort of retaliations.

From Far And Wide

Not just to the horizon, but beyond creeds, protests and symbols with an insight and understanding for all.

O Canada, We Stand On Guard For Thee

Not that we want to flaunt our strength but to be capable of facing the strongest should that enemy appear.

God Keep Our Land Glorious and Free

That means justice. The principles and qualities of dealing fairly with others.

O Canada We Stand On Guard For Thee

We protect all doctrines and share our spirit with logic and reason.

O Canada We Stand On Guard For Thee

So we can say to a neighbor, it's as much my country as it is yours.

It took courage and daring for Bernie Legge to come to Canada, but come he did. And two generations later, we relish and cherish his courageous decision.

There's a bit more to all of this, and please excuse me if I remain in a patriotic mode for a moment or two more.

Every year when Remembrance Day comes around, I make it my business to attend the November 11 ceremonies in New Westminster, where my dad first arrived in British Columbia. I do it not just because he served in the risky business of wartime maritime transportation, and as a warden during the blitz of London, but for a greater reason—to remember *everyone* who fought and died for our freedom.

The way I look at it, showing up once a year to bow my head and remember all of those images and all of those heroes is the very least I can do in this glorious and free land.

A lady called Edna Anderson, who served as Poet Laureate for New Westminster a year ago, also remembered all of these things, and read about them in her poem to the Remembrance Day crowd on that chilly November day.

> . . . The eleventh hour, eleventh day,
> Eleventh month, down through the years,
> We stand proudly, while bugles play!
> Knowing not their suffering or their fears;
> Our proud hearts are sad, but we'll carry on,
> We see all this, each year, despite our tears.

I got a letter in the mail early in the summer of 2000, a circular from one James C. Dobson, Ph.D., who is president of an organization called Focus on the Family. Among other things, Dr. Dobson talked about John Lukacs' recently published book, "Five Days in London: May, 1940."

I haven't read the book, but according to Dr. Dobson it tells the story of some of the things that were happening in London in the Second World War's darkest days—when it seemed entirely likely that Hitler's armies, already on a roll, would sweep into Britain and change the world forever.

I'll pick up on some of Dr. Dobson's telling of the story, which I found most interesting.

" . . . on May 24, 1940, a half-million British and French soldiers were huddled hopelessly at Dunkirk, waiting for inevitable death or imprisonment. It was at that desperate moment that the churches in Britain called for a national day of prayer. It had been suggested during April, but the Archbishop of Canterbury had opposed it. He said he didn't want the call to prayer to be misinterpreted, whatever that meant. But with the alarming deterioration of the military situation in France, he and many others decided that it was, indeed, time to pray. On May 23, numerous political leaders, newspaper editors and King George VI issued a call for a national day of prayer to be held on Sunday, May 26.

"No one could have anticipated what was to happen during those three momentous days. Just 24 hours after the call for prayer, Adolf Hitler inexplicably ordered his armies to halt, to the surprise and dismay of even his own generals. Two days later, on May 26, the nation gathered to pray. Church attendance skyrocketed, including a large gathering at Westminster Abbey, during which people pleaded with the Almighty to spare their husbands, sons and fathers at Dunkirk.

"Former Prime Minister Neville Chamberlain wrote this in his diary: 'May 26. Blackest day of all . . . This was the National Day of Prayer.' In reality, it turned out to be one of the most dramatic turning points of the war. At seven o'clock that evening, a critical order was issued to attempt a desperate evacuation of Dunkirk. Every tiny vessel and private craft was sent across the Channel with orders to rescue as many men as possible before the arrival of the Germans.

"Hitler's armies remained largely in place not only on the 24th, 25th and 26th, but, incredibly, until early June. To this day, no one knows exactly why. The Fuhrer held victory in the palm of his hand, and yet he prevented his combat troops from finishing the job."

Why did it happen the way it did? Dr. Dobson says that Hitler's armies "were halted by the same God who shut the mouths of the lions during Daniel's night of peril. Just as the Lord heard the prayers of the Israelites so long ago, I believe He was listening when hundreds of thousands of believers in the U.K. were praying for divine intervention.

"For nine critical days, the Germans were content to shell and bomb Dunkirk from the air and from a distance. Meanwhile, large numbers of Allied soldiers were scrambling aboard little boats to be taken to safety in England. On May 29, 47,000 were rescued; on May 30, 53,000; on May 31,

68,000; on June 1, 64,000. In all, 336,000 men found their way to safety . . . The British leaders were jubilant—and astounded."

John Lukacs wrote that then Prime Minister Churchill succeeded "because of his resolution and—allow me to say this—because of God's will, of which, like every human being, (Churchill) was but an instrument. He was surely no saint, he was not a religious man, and he had many faults. Yet so it happened."

Indeed it did. And because of the Dunkirk miracle—how quickly 60 years have flown!—and all that followed it, we live different lives.

Where I live, I am able to relish the kind of peace and freedom that not only permits me to pursue every conceivable avenue of endeavor, but also to wear a poppy, to show up every November 11 in New Westminster, bow my head for a moment, and say thank you.

Did prayer stop the advancing German army?

God only knows.

CHAPTER 9

Fathers

WHILE THIS WILL END UP BEING a chapter about fathers, I had
some material that I like that didn't seem to fit anywhere else,
so as I often do when I'm making corporate presentations, I
will open with some stuff that will make you comfortable,
and perhaps prompt a smile.

Making speeches, I travel a lot, and because I'm always
in need of new and interesting material, I keep my eyes and

ears open. As well as making anecdotal notes about situations and characters that enter my on-the-road life, I read labels, and keep a record of the best. If it's good enough for Andy Rooney, it's good enough for me.

On a hair dryer in a hotel room in Atlanta were the words: "Do not use while sleeping." Hey, I wouldn't *dream* of it! On a bar of soap in Toronto it said: "Directions: Use like regular soap." Huh? On a frozen dinner in a British supermarket: "Serving suggestions: Defrost." Begin at the beginning. On a tiramisu dessert were the words: "Do not turn upside down." The message, perhaps not surprisingly, was printed on the bottom of the box. A pudding from Marks & Spencer in England had these helpful words of instruction: "Product will be hot after heating." Included with instructions for an iron? "Do not iron clothes on body."

When our kids were younger, we would often holiday in England. I remember buying some children's cough medicine that included the words: "Do not drive car or operate machinery." There was nothing about getting a licence! A bottle of Nytol, which is supposed to help you sleep, warned: "May cause drowsiness." I'll take two!

On a string of Christmas lights: "For indoor or outdoor use only." But nowhere else! In Japan, we picked up a food processor with the obtuse warning: "Do not be used for the other use." Wouldn't dream of it. On a package of airline peanuts? "Instructions: Open packet, eat nuts." And while this one is not mine, it must be included. On a Swedish chainsaw, it said: "Do not attempt to stop chain with your hand." Use your head?

Enough of that. Change of thought.

A father was pushing a baby buggy along the high street and a friend came over and asked him what he had in the buggy.

"That's my new baby boy." And the friend said: "How about this? I'll give you a million dollars for that boy." And the proud father said: "Are you kidding? There's not enough money in the world for *this* baby."

Sixteen years later, the two meet again on the street. And the friend says, "Hey, how's your million-dollar kid?" And the father says, "Million bucks? I wouldn't give you a plugged nickel for that kid." Hmmm.

I don't know who Mrs. Nolte is, but she wrote some marvellous words called, "Children Learn What They Live." And they went something like this:

If children live with criticism, they learn to condemn.
If children live with hostility, they learn to fight.
If children live with fear, they learn to be apprehensive.
If children live with pity, they learn to feel sorry for
    themselves.
If children live with jealousy, they learn what envy is.
If children live with shame, they learn to feel guilty.
If children live with encouragement, they learn to be
    confident.

If children live with tolerance, they learn to be patient.

If children live with praise, they learn to be appreciative.

If children live with approval, they learn to like
themselves.

If children live with recognition, they learn that it is good
to have a goal.

If children live with sharing, they learn about generosity.

If children live with honesty and fairness, they learn about
truth and justice.

If children live with security, they learn to have faith in
themselves and in those about them.

If children live with friendliness, they learn that a world is
a nice place to live.

If children live with serenity, your child and my child's
children will live with peace of mind.

When I was asked to prepare a tribute to fathers for a corporate audience in Germany in the spring of 2000, the date of the presentation was the second anniversary of the death of my own father. I remember that day well. I had a call from the hospital to tell me that my father was near death, that my wife and our three children should come soon to say our last farewells.

Dad had been in the hospital for almost a month battling lung cancer, and we were blessed that day that Nurse Ruth Stevens was on duty, and that it was she who had called. In his last weeks Nurse Stevens had spent much time with dad, and we knew that he would be in good hands in the last difficult part of his life. In less than 20 minutes, my wife and three girls were at his bedside. We shared private thoughts and prayers in those final moments, and then, taking his last cue—the theatre had been his life—he slipped away.

My heart broke, and all five of us wept as in that moment we entered a new life passage. My dad had been a fantastic father, an amazing husband, and a loving and caring grandfather. A leader in his New Westminster, B.C. community, and an inspiration to anyone who met him, I found it easy to tell his story in "If Only I'd Said That," my most recent book. It helped me to keep his memory alive.

From a little book called "Tact" that he always carried in his pocket, my dad often shared its philosophy—thoughts that guided his own life.

"Son," he said, "never accept success or failure because neither need to be permanent."

"Consider the possibilities, not the limitations."

"Be enthusiastic, see the good, expect the best, be prepared for change."

"Failure to prepare is preparing to fail."

"Treat people with love and respect and they in return will treat you with love and respect."

"Be considerate in every word and act; cultivate tolerance towards others; patiently listen to opinions which oppose yours; and above all never lose your temper."

"The great prizes of life do not fall to the most brilliant, to the cleverest, to the shrewdest, or to the best educated. They fall to the most level-headed, to those who are sound in judgment. In any large organization, whether it be the church, family, or business, when a man is wanted for a responsible position, his shrewdness is not considered as important as the quality of his judgment."

"Nothing in the world can take the place of persistence. Talent will not. Nothing is more common than unsuccessful men with talent. Genius will not. Unrewarded genius is almost a proverb. Education will not. The world is full of educated derelicts. You need persistence, patience and a push. The bulldog's claim to fame is based on a single quality. He can hang on."

It was on a subsequent Father's Day that I delivered a Tribute to Fathers, and I told my audience that I am a proud father of three wonderful daughters who I love with all my heart. They were in the audience as I spoke.

I put an acronym together for the word father.

"F," I said, is for being faithful, making a commitment and fulfilling promises. We all make commitments and promises. And we always say that we'll be faithful. But too often we break promises to the ones we love the most.

I was on a speaking assignment in Tucson a few years ago. It was a Thursday, and I knew that on the following evening I was due to attend my daughter's graduation dinner in Vancouver. I'd made that promise. On the Friday morning I was at Tucson airport at 6:30 to catch my flight home. At seven, no plane. And no plane at 7:30. At eight, I was advised that the flight from Dallas to Tucson had been cancelled because of bad weather, "but we can get you home sometime tomorrow."

I thought to myself: "But I made a promise. It's graduation." There was no other way but to charter a jet to Los Angeles to connect with a flight north. It cost a heap of money, but it was worth every nickel to be there, to come through, to be the kind of dad I knew I aspired to be.

Another story. There was a father who said to his son: "No matter what, I'll be there for you." It was in Armenia. And one morning, after he had taken his son to school, there was an earthquake that flattened the city and took the lives of 30,000 people. The father didn't die, and in the aftermath of the quake, he found his way back to where he remembered leaving his son. The school had been destroyed, but he somehow figured where the classroom might be and started digging. The authorities came over and told him to stop, warned of potential dangers.

The father said: "Are you going to help me, or is this my responsibility?" Despite the warnings and lack of help, the father dug. For eight hours, 16, 24, 36 hours. And then he heard a voice saying: "Dad, is that you?" "Son," said the father, "it's you!" "Yes," said the boy. "There's 12 of us down here. And I told them that if my dad survived the earthquake, no matter what, he will be there for me." So the father said: "Son, come on out." "No," said the boy. "Take the others first. I'm O.K. I knew you'd come for me."

"A" is for attitude, for action and activity. I have a great relationship with my three daughters. We're not only father and daughters, we're also best friends. I told a guy once that we always go on holidays as a family, and we've done it forever. "You're telling me that your oldest daughter is 30 years old, and you're taking them away on a holiday in August? Are you nuts? I wouldn't take my kid across the room, let alone on holidays."

I said: "But they *want* to go. You kind of missed the point. We're in love with each other. We're committed to one another. This is nothing new." And I saw in his face a look of awe, and maybe even some kind of regret.

In all of the activities that I have been involved in, the charity work that I do, and in my own golf tournament, my girls have been there with me. They've been hostesses. They've taken money. They've sold my books. They've played in the golf tournament. Ever since they were little kids, they've been around their dad, and their dad has been around them. "A" is for attitude, action and activity. Be involved. Get them involved with you.

"T" is for thankfulness and tenderness. I said to Amanda: "If I were to say thankfulness and tenderness, what would come to your mind?" And she said, "Oh dad, our Sunday dinners. It's tough to get a word in edgewise because we're all laughing so much. We're all having such a great time. That's all about thankfulness and tenderness."

We say, "I love you" to one another every day. On the phone I say, "I love you, sweetheart." And we hug a lot. They've never shied away from a hug. No matter when or where. When I dropped them off at school, a hug and a kiss. I am thankful for that relationship. I am thankful for the tenderness that God gave my three girls and me.

"H" is for humor and the heart of love. Another story that I've told many times. Canada is considered by the United Nations to be the only country that is officially bilingual, and my middle daughter, Rebecca, wanted to speak French, the second official language. So when she was in grade six, we enrolled her in French Immersion, and she remained there until graduation, at which time we all figured that she was well and truly bilingual. But every time we went to French-speaking Quebec, the locals would always answer her in English, which made all of us, including Rebecca, doubt whether she was indeed bilingual. Then she had this great idea. Dad, she said, I need to go to university in France. Then I'll really know!

So she saved the money and in September of that year, I took her to the airport to board a British Airways flight to Heathrow that would connect to a flight to Nice. Her flight left at eight and at about 7:35 I said: "Sweetheart, it's time to go." And she dropped her knapsack and her books, threw her arms around me and said: "Dad, I love you so much, even if I'm scared to death." So I gave her a credit card. And I said that if anything went wrong in Nice, she could take the card down to British Airways, no questions asked, and fly home.

But before she got on the plane, there was more. My dad always taught me that if you want to be successful, you have to be creative, resourceful and inventive—do what's required. And somewhere along the way, these points were passed on to *my* kids, and Rebecca said: "Dad, why don't you get a speaking engagement in London halfway through my year, fly me up from Nice, and we'll spend the weekend together."

I said, "What a great idea!" And she said, "I've even picked the weekend." So as I drove home from the airport, I thought of nothing else but how do I get a speaking engagement in London? On the Monday before I was due to be in London, I got an engagement in the Bahamas. It's not quite London, but it's on the way. Then on the Tuesday of that week, I got an engagement in New York. Heck, I said, I'm halfway there. Then I had another idea. I had lots of points with all of this flying, so I said to wife Kay and daughters Samantha and Amanda: "Why don't you guys come over with me and we'll surprise Rebecca." Kay and Amanda couldn't come; they were in the middle of final exams. But Sam was working downtown and she jumped at the idea. So

I said, "I'll meet you in London." Sam and I met beneath Big Ben on the Thursday and headed back to the hotel to await the arrival from France of Rebecca.

While we were waiting, I got friendly with the hotel's night manager, a delightful lady called Anna Pona. And being resourceful, creative and inventive, I said: "Anna, how about this for an idea? This is Samantha, my eldest daughter. She's flown over from Vancouver, and I've come over from New York. My middle daughter Rebecca is flying up from university in the south of France. She doesn't know this daughter is here. Because Samantha and Rebecca haven't seen each other for a while, wouldn't it be fun for Samantha to be behind the counter to check Rebecca in?" And Anna said, "Great idea. Let's do it!"

In due course, a black London cab pulled up at the front door and Rebecca got out. I threw my arms around her, and we just kind of hugged and cried. And I said: "You know, sweetheart, you can't stay in a room with dad anymore. But I got you a room, an adjoining room. Let's check in."

Sam, meanwhile, after totally confusing the hotel's manager by being in the office behind the registration desk, emerged in a makeshift uniform to assume her new duties.

Rebecca walked up to the desk to register, and smiling Samantha said: "Good afternoon miss, may I please see your passport?"

"Passport, pass . . . wow, you look exactly like my sister Sama . . . Sam, it's *you*! It's *you*!"

Sam jumped over the counter and there we were, the three of us. And the hugs went on and on. And out of the corner of my eye, I could see Anna Pona, the manager of the hotel, and a handful of other smiling staff members observing a love affair going on in the lobby, a love affair that had been going on for a lifetime.

"H" is for humor, the heart of love and memories.

"E" is for encouragement and enthusiasm. My dad encouraged not only me, but my wife Kay, and all of my daughters. I hope that I've also done that for them—encouraged everything that they have wanted to do. I haven't always *agreed* with everything they'd wanted to do, in which cases I fervently prayed that at some point they would come to their senses. But regardless of the direction that their lives may take them, I have always let them know that they are loved unconditionally.

And "R" is for respect and love. If you want respect, you have to give respect. If you want them to love you, you have to love them. You have to listen to what they have to say and work very hard at never treating them as children. One little deal that I have with my girls is that we have agreed among the four of us that when a boy comes along and wants to marry any one of them, he has no option but to phone me and invite me for lunch, alone. And somewhere during that lunch, he will ask me for my daughter's hand in marriage.

They are scared to death. But they know I love my girls. They know I respect my girls. They know that if they want to marry them, they're going to have to do lunch. So "R" is for respect and love. And there *were* lunches. And Samantha and Amanda are now married.

Some years ago, when they were all living at home, I put down some words that I called My Three Sleeping Beauties, and these were the words:

I tiptoed into your room tonight. I looked at you smiling in your sleep. You were so lovely my heart nearly broke. And I thought how very much like Sleeping Beauty a little girl is. When I tucked you in, I never knew how old you'd be when you awoke. One evening you'd crawl into dad's lap and throw your arms around his neck, and the next morning you might be too grown up for that sort of thing.

You are so quickly approaching the awkward age, too young to drive the car, too old to be carried in the house on daddy's shoulder.

I have a secret that I've never told you, Sleeping Beauty. You're going on an exciting trip.

You will travel from yesterday all the way to tomorrow. It's a rapid journey and you'll travel light, leaving behind your measles, freckles, lumps, bumps, bubble gum and me.

I promise not to feel hurt when you discover the world is a lot more interesting than your daddy's lap.

Yesterday you wore blue jeans and your hair was in pigtails. Tomorrow you will be in blue gingham, and your hair will be in a ponytail. You will view the world from a lofty pair of high-heeled shoes.

Yesterday you could fix your Cabbage Patch Kids with a hug.

Tomorrow you will be able to break a boy's heart with a kiss.

Yesterday you could get lost one aisle away from me in the supermarket, and now I have to worry about losing you down another aisle to a strange young man.

Just at the point when your growing pains stop, mine begin.

Yesterday, you were a pain in the neck when you were around. And tomorrow, you will be an ache in my heart when you're not.

Tomorrow you'll lay aside your jump rope to tie up the telephone line and the little boy that pushed you into the mud will fight to have a dance with you.

The clock downstairs is counting the minutes for you.

The sky upstairs is saving its brightest stars, the sun is waiting with its shiniest day.

I can't expect you to live in your dollhouse forever.

Sooner or later the butterfly sheds the cocoon. And the smallest bird must try its wings.

When you grow up and out of my arms.

When you finally get too big for my shirts, I shall recall how you scattered dust and dolls in every room in the house and that you spread sunshine too.

The dust has settled. Your mother's picked up the dolls, but the sunshine will always fill the corners of our hearts.

So here I am, talking while you sleep, because if you saw this look on my face, you'd laugh. And if I spoke with this lump in my throat, I'd cry.

Yes, my daughters, when I looked at you tonight you were Sleeping Beauty. And so I tiptoed over and I kissed you. You didn't wake up. I knew that you wouldn't. But according to the legend, only the handsome young prince can open your eyes and I am just the father of the future brides. Slumber on, my darlings. Tomorrow when you wake, you'll be young ladies. And you won't even realize you've changed courses in the middle of your dreams. But you might notice a change in me. I'll look different somehow, a little sadder, a little wiser, but a lot richer.

Tonight I kiss three princesses and I feel like a king.

O to be a dad. O to be blessed with three children like mine. O to be thankful to my heavenly Father for his graciousness, for his love. And for the gifts that he gave to *my* father.

It's an awesome responsibility to be a dad. And a dad's greatest gift to his children is unconditional love.

CHAPTER 10

Attitude Is Everything

A LOT HAS BEEN WRITTEN about the importance of positive attitude.

I didn't write that "your attitude determines your altitude." But if I'd picked up a buck for every time I've quoted it, read it, and heard it on audio and video training tapes, I would be rich indeed.

Here's something to think about. I submit that the quality

that business leaders need more than almost any other is a positive attitude. Not a Pollyanna, Mary Poppins kind of attitude, but a rich, positive attitude that is engaging, that lets others know that you are a person of significance. A person with a positive attitude brightens a room not by leaving it, but by entering it.

I've said this many times, but for my money the Number One motivational speaker in the last 50 years was Earl Nightingale, a practical, common sense kind of guy, whose messages always struck a receptive chord. Earl called attitude the "Magic Word."

The magic word is a two-edged sword. It brings us the success we seek, or if misused, a life of disappointment and frustration. Knowledge and understanding of this key word is Step Number One on your journey to greater success. It's the foundation upon which to build a happier, healthier, more prosperous life for you and your family.

Attitude. The Magic Word! When it comes to the results we expect in life, experts call it the most important word in this or any other language.

Attitude is defined as the position or bearing as indicating action, feeling, or mood. And it is our actions, feelings and moods which will determine the actions, feelings or moods that others have for us.

Our attitude toward *life* will determine life's attitude toward *us*. And what does this mean? Everything functions by a law of cause and effect. Which is why I say that success can be guaranteed—and will come to us every time, if we live in the right manner. We are charged with producing causes. The effects or the rewards of our actions will take care of themselves.

Good attitude means good results. Fair attitude, fair results. Bad attitude, bad results.

William James of Harvard University put it this way: "The greatest discovery of my generation is that human beings can alter their lives by altering their attitudes of mind."

I spoke recently at a Toastmasters International convention in St. Louis, Missouri, the "show me" state. It was an evening presentation to about 1,800 men and women from around the world. The Adams Mark Hotel was picked for the convention, and I had the honor of being the keynote speaker on opening night.

Earlier in the day I went to get my shoes shined in the basement of the hotel. A man in his late sixties was doing a great job of making my shoes look like new. He had a huge nametag on his lapel with inch-high letters that spelled out the name SHED. To make conversation I asked: "Is that your real name, or just a nickname?" He pulled back, clapped his hands together and smiled: "My name is SHED. My momma named me SHED."

"Wow," I thought. Here's a guy with a good attitude.

"Shed, I notice you have a stethoscope around your neck. What's that for?" He raised his arm to hold the stethoscope, and said: "I am a doctor of shoes, and I ain't lost a patient in

37 years. In fact, you could say I've been saving soles for almost four decades."

I then noticed a sign on the side of his stand that said: "If you've got a good attitude, I charge you $2. If you've got a bad attitude, I charge you $6. Because it costs to have a bad attitude."

This man who had shone shoes for 37 years taught me much about the importance of good attitude.

No matter what you do in life, if you have a positive attitude, you'll always be 100 per cent. According to our alphabet system, if you assign a numerical value to each letter on the alphabet scale of 26, attitude will equal 100 per cent. Coincidence of course, but something to remember.

A	=	1
T	=	20
T	=	20
I	=	9
T	=	20
U	=	21
D	=	4
E	=	5

ATTITUDE	100

W. Clement Stone once said: " I can't guarantee you'll be successful with a positive attitude, but I can guarantee you won't be successful with a negative attitude."

In Keith Harrell's book "Attitude is Everything," he says: "You can build a strong and powerful body with exercise, but it takes commitment and hard work. You have the same power to build a positive attitude with mental exercises. This too takes commitment, hard work and continuous effort."

In a survey of 100 of the Fortune 500 companies, the question was asked: "Why did you fire the last 10,000 people you fired?" And the answer came back that 9,700 were fired because of their attitude, because they couldn't get along with others.

One of my favorite affirmations of all of these came from Pastor Chuck Swindoll.

It is simply called Attitudes, and it goes like this:

"The longer I live, the more I realize the impact of attitude on life. Attitude to me is more important than facts, it is more important than the past, than education, than money, than circumstances, than failures, than successes, than what other people think or say or do. It is more important than appearance, giftedness or skill. It will make or break a company, a church, a home. The remarkable thing is we have a choice every day regarding the attitude we will embrace for that day. We cannot change our past; we cannot change the fact that people will act in a certain way. We cannot change the inevitable. The only thing we can do is play on the one string we have, and that is our attitude. I am convinced that life is 10 per cent what happens to me and 90 per cent how I react to it. And so it is with you. We are in charge of our attitudes!"

Thank you, Pastor Chuck. Truer words were never spoken.

According to Harvard University, 85 per cent of the reason a person gets a job and gets ahead in that job is that he or she has the right mental attitude.

A classic study at Harvard Medical School followed graduates for 50 years after they graduated, allowing a rare opportunity to follow the effect of positive thinking over almost an entire lifetime.

Those who handled life with humor, altruism and positive thinking went on to lead much more successful and healthy lives. By the age of 60, very few of this group were chronically ill.

Fully one-third of those who were pessimistic in their thinking showed poor health by age 60.

If you want to feel positive, act positive.

If you want to feel happy, act happy.

If you want to feel optimistic, act optimistic.

If you want . . . You get the idea.

In Brian Tracy's latest book, titled "The 100 Absolutely Unbreakable Laws of Business Success," optimism is the foundation of a positive attitude. Brian Tracy thinks this is so important it is Law No. 39, The Law of Optimism.

The more optimistic and positive you are, the calmer, more positive and more creative you will be. And in his book "The Wealth & Poverty of Nations," after a truly spectacular review of a thousand years of economic history, David Landes ends with these words: "In this world, the optimists have it, not because they are always right, but because they are always positive. Even when wrong, they are positive and that is the way of achievement, correction, improvement and success. The one lesson that emerges is the need to keep trying."

Dare to have a positive attitude for 30 days, then repeat the exercise every 30 days for a year. It won't hurt a bit, and your sphere of influence will astound you.

No question at all that you'll be a lot closer to winning at home, at work, in your community—and in life!

CHAPTER 11

Dosen

IF YOU WATCHED THE VARIETY CLUB TELETHON in British Columbia a few years ago, you may have seen me interview Mike Dosen. Mike presented me with a cheque for $4,000 for the special needs kids in Variety's British Columbia world.

For more than 35 years, the Variety Club Telethon has been broadcast live for 22 hours in the middle of February on

British Columbia Television, and has raised more than $70 million. All of this money has been spent in British Columbia to help children who depend on others to make their lives meaningful, and to help them to attempt to enjoy the kind of life that most of us take for granted.

These kids dare to win every day of their lives, combatting obstacles that are unimaginable to you and me. Having been part of Variety's Telethon as a co-host for 20 years, and having interviewed countless individuals and receiving hundreds of cheques for Variety, interviewing Mike Dosen—who you don't yet know—may seem quite normal.

Let me tell you his story.

In January of 1998, Ron Loftus, the owner and editor of a weekly newspaper in the Interior British Columbia community of Oliver, called me and said he was doing a piece on Variety Telethon and was interviewing Mike Dosen.

Mike, he told me, was dying, and his wish as his health worsened, was to present his modest personal fundraising cheque live on the telethon. Ron asked if I might help make it happen.

I said: "Have him drive to Vancouver, and I'll get him on this year's show and he can present his cheque to me live."

And Ron replied: "Pete, you don't understand. Mike is in his sixties, he's a quadriplegic, barely speaks, can only move his head, is confined to a huge wheelchair and requires 24-hour medical supervision."

"How on earth does he raise the money?"

And Ron said: "He gets his nurses to drive him to Penticton, and in his motorized wheelchair, he drives up and down the streets and asks."

"But Ron, you said he can barely speak?"

"He has a tin can and a sign that does his talking for him. It says Give to the Kids of Variety."

"And how many years has he been doing this?"

"This is his fourth year."

"And how much has he raised?"

Ron guessed and said: "In the first year, about $500, the second year about $950, the third year he raised over $2,000. We don't know how well he's doing this year. He hasn't finished."

It sounded incredible, a story of triumph over substantial tragedy. I told him I'd do my best, and pitched the idea to Shel Piercy, Variety's brilliant Telethon producer. We talked about flying Mike to Vancouver on Telethon weekend and interviewing him live as he presented us with his cheque.

It was then that we discovered the magnitude of that decision. The size of his wheelchair and equipment, his oxygen tank, nurses, hoists on and off the plane, medical procedures to protect Mike—it was more than a daunting task and one which turned out to be full of risks and dangers for Mike. We quickly ruled it out as impractical.

I said to myself: "Be creative, inventive, resourceful. Dare to dream."

I called his nurse and said, "Can you get Mike to

Kelowna?" It's a couple of hours from Mike's hometown. She said she could.

I arranged for a private jet to fly the producer, sound person, cameraman, makeup person and assistant to Kelowna. We would interview Mike in the Okanagan's Apple Museum, which was donated for the event.

Mike and his nurse were there right on time. His big day had come and he was grinning from ear to ear, knowing that he would be on the Telethon to personally present us with his cheque. The interview lasted for about three minutes. I kissed Mike on the forehead, thanked him for his courageous effort, and we all climbed into the jet to head back to the coast, a band of sadder, wiser people.

Everyone in Mike's hospital watched the Telethon, waiting for the piece that Shel Piercy had carefully edited for the final hour of the show. It really *was* a powerful finale, and we were collectively proud that we had been able to fulfill the wish of a courageous man who had spent 40 years a prisoner of a wheelchair.

But as radio man Paul Harvey would say: "Now for the other half of the story."

Shortly after that year's Telethon, Mike was transferred to Queen's Park Hospital in New Westminster, on the coast, and a long way from his Interior B.C. home. I was aware of his arrival, as I was then Honorary Chairman of the Hospital Board. Mike was still talking about his moment of Telethon fame. Physically, he was fading, but the memory of those moments remained, and I guess it was logical that a call would go out for me to come to the hospital to say hello.

But by the time word reached me, Mike had died. His niece called and asked if I could come to the funeral.

"Of course I'll be there," I said.

"Toward the end," she said, "all Mike could talk about was his appearance on the Telethon."

I made plans to be at the funeral in plenty of time, figuring there would be lots of people there to say farewell. I arrived for the 1 p.m. event at 12:05, and found a seat at the back of the empty sanctuary. Mike was in an open coffin, and the pain and suffering he'd experienced for 40 years had left his face. He really looked at peace and I knew he was in a better place.

For 20 minutes I sat alone waiting for the crowds. At 12:45, it was still just Mike and me. At 12:50, the same. Then at 12:55, six people came into the funeral home—two brothers and their wives, the niece who had called me, and the minister. That was it. Six people, and me in the back row.

I cried at the loneliness of it all.

I smiled too because we had been able to make this man's dying wish come true. Hundreds of thousands of television viewers had been there to cheer him on.

On the streets of Penticton, and certainly in our collective hearts, we will remember Mike Dosen as a man who dared and won!

CHAPTER 12

The Rocket

HISTORY WILL JUDGE the worth of the Internet, but while we wait for that decision, let me say that I am delighted to have been around when it came into being, and to have had the chance to realize just some of what I know is its enormous potential.

News, e-mail, commerce, it's all there, along with what seems to be the world's greatest data bank of information.

I have absolutely no idea how many times in my life that I have called or visited a library or flipped open a book to source information that I needed for whatever reason. But I do know that in this search I have sometimes been frustrated because time, or available timely reference works just didn't permit me to get the answers I needed when I needed them.

The Internet, on the other hand, is right there—as complete and as timely as I could ever want, the source for just about everything. Hit the Search button, and you've got it!

In June of 2000, right after the death of Maurice "Rocket" Richard, I was contracted to make a presentation that would extol the style and virtues of a local man whose life and work seemed to embody many of the qualities that had propelled the Rocket in *his* great life. And not having all of the facts on this Canadian hockey legend at hand, I dived into the Web to find out more.

What a fascinating collection of material was waiting for me. What inspirational stuff!

How about this as a for-instance, gleaned from an address called *History & People: Canadian Personalities.* And I thank the site and its authors for this information.

"December 28, 1944 was moving day for 23-year-old Maurice Richard. All day he hefted furniture, including a piano, into his new house. That night he scored five goals and three assists to lead the Montreal Canadiens to a 9-1 victory over the Detroit Red Wings, setting an NHL record."

Here's another one from the same source:

"During Game Seven of the 1952 Stanley Cup final against Boston, an injured Richard, squinting through blood from an earlier blow, scored the tie-breaking goal to win the Cup. He received a four-minute standing ovation, the longest in Montreal Forum history."

And more:

"Rocket Richard's explosive 18-year career made him the most exciting player of his generation, and a national hero. Fiercely competitive, a virtual demon on ice, Richard was a scoring genius. In 1944-45 he scored 50 goals in 50 games, hockey's most celebrated record for many years. He led the league in goals five times and won the Hart Trophy in 1947. Above all, Richard excelled under pressure. He scored 18 playoff game-winning goals, still a record today.

"Richard's passionate personality, combined with his short temper, often led to conflict, and once, to a riot. In March 1955, in the fury of a hockey fight, Richard punched a linesman. When President Clarence Campbell suspended Richard for the rest of the season, Montreal fans were outraged.

"The next night Campbell dared to show up at the game, and the fans went wild. They attacked Campbell, and the violence spilled out onto the streets in the worst riot in Canadian sports history.

"Richard's career ended in 1960 after he suffered a severed Achilles tendon. Yet despite missing many games due to injuries over his career, The Rocket scored 544 goals in regular season play, and 82 goals in Stanley Cup play. He was named Canada's male athlete of the year twice, and to many Quebecois he remains the 'man of the century.' Maurice Richard passed away on May 27, 2000, after losing his second battle with cancer."

And what did his peers and others say about the Rocket? The Associated Press jumped to the phones immediately after Richard's death, and in that moment, this is what some of them said, again recorded for posterity on a web site.

Hockey broadcaster Dick Irvin Jr., whose father coached Richard, said: "I have a theory: Whenever he scored a goal, the cheer at the Forum was just a decibel higher than when anybody else scored, no matter the importance."

Former Penguins star Mario Lemieux: "He was one of the best players who ever played in the history of hockey."

Quebec Premier Lucien Bouchard: "He had a solid will to win and was a tireless worker. Skilled and determined, he was in all respects an indispensable teammate and a formidable opponent."

Ronald Corey, former president of the Canadiens: "There wasn't a dry eye in the house when he received a standing ovation at the closing of the Montreal Forum [in 1996]. It was extremely moving; I almost fell to the ground, my knees were trembling so hard."

Canadian Prime Minister Jean Chrétien: "What truly set him apart, what made him a special hero to the fans, was his extraordinary intensity. He played with great emotion and flair and possessed an unmatched will to win. His dazzling combination of skill and drive not only made him one of the greatest hockey players ever, it also made him a symbol to all of what it takes to be a true champion."

Former Detroit great Gordie Howe: "He could rile up the Montreal fans in a hurry. God, sometimes I felt sorry for the man. He must have got a standing ovation when he went shopping."

And then there was a quote that I really liked. It came from former Canadiens star Guy Lafleur, and he said:

"We all wanted to wear [his] No. 9 when we were kids—not just me. This man played a role in my career through the pride he displayed each time he wore the sweater of the Montreal Canadiens."

Lafleur's initial memory echoed those of other nameless people in the street. One of them said: "When we played kid hockey on the outdoor rinks of Montreal, our entire team wore Montreal Canadiens sweaters. All of them had No. 9 on the back. And so did everyone on the other team!"

Both teams were wearing red, white and blue Montreal Canadiens uniforms. All with the No. 9. All with the name Richard.

They *all* wanted to be like their hero Rocket Richard. Nice idea, but absolute chaos on the ice if you didn't know absolutely everyone in a personal, in-your-face way!

I thought about all of this when I began to put this chapter together, and how I had used the information I gathered on the Rocket to make my presentation a month after he died.

The members of the best teams can't really be effective if everyone has the same kind of talent. It's terrific to have a Rocket on your side, but you need all of the others to be there so the Rocket and the team can shine. You need strong forwards and a strong defence; you need centres and good guys on the wing; you need an impenetrable goalie. Collectively, it's a team.

We can't all be Rocket Richards, but we can still be players. Some of us can skate faster, some can shoot harder, some can pass better. Individually, we *all* count.

The brilliance of Rocket Richard inspired his team, the fans, and all of the kids who wanted to wear his treasured No. 9 sweater.

Your individual brilliance can do the same in *your* circle of influence. Unique *you* can strengthen and influence positive change in teams of all kinds—in your family, your office, your community, your country, and your world. We all count. We can all dare and win.

That's what I said in my presentation.

And I thank the Web and the Rocket for my inspiration.

Everyone who chooses to make Canada their new home is seduced along the way by the power of hockey. Even an ex-Brit like me! At a Vancouver Canucks home game last season I easily coaxed myself into purchasing two pieces of art that seemed appropriate to include with this chapter. My first was a limited edition print that portrayed two youngsters facing off in an impromptu game. The lads are Montreal's Guy Lafleur and Toronto's Darryl Sittler. And the print was signed by both of them.

When Maurice (Rocket) Richard died, Guy Lafleur said that when he played kid hockey on the outdoor rinks of Montreal, both teams wore Montreal Canadiens sweaters and all of them had No. 9— the Rocket's Number—on the back. All the kids wanted to be like the Rocket. He was king of the game and he will endure forever as the definitive icon of hockey. This picture of the Rocket and his brother Henri was my second purchase at the Canucks game.

CHAPTER 13

A Dozen Quickies

An Even Dozen

This chapter will be a quick read of a dozen stories that I always keep close enough to help me kick-start what may be shaping up as a dull day.

No. 1

The Lowdown on Luck

It is sometimes suggested that one of my super salespeople at Canada Wide Magazines is lucky. Not so, he says. "I get up two hours earlier than the other salespeople, and I work two hours longer than my colleagues. What I do is give luck the opportunity to find *me*."

I have found that the harder I work, the luckier I get. What we call luck comes when we maximize the time we have to be productive. Sorry, but the only place luck comes before work is in the dictionary.

No. 2

Success Defined

I've heard two great definitions of success. Earl Nightingale said that success is nothing more than the pursuit of a worthy ideal. Nido Qubein defined success as balance.

Unless you have balance in your life you can't be truly successful. If you have all the money in the world and no one likes you, wants to marry you, or be with you, you aren't successful. Similarly, if you have a happy marriage and a comfortable home, but can't sleep because you can't make the mortgage payments, you are out of balance. Pursue a worthy ideal and keep your life in balance. That's success!

No. 3

Are you willing to pay the price?

Texas oil billionaire Bunker Hunt said: "Success is simple. First, you decide exactly what you want in life. Second, you decide whether you're willing to pay the price to make it happen—and then you pay the price. Many successful people . . . pay the price to get there. But don't pay the price to stay."

Here's a question. What qualities, work ethics and attitudes got you to where you are today?

No. 4

Are you unforgettable?

I loved what the King of Siam said in the *Anna and the King* movie with Jodie Foster—and I wrote it down in the dark: "It is always surprising how small a part of life is taken up by meaningful moments. Most of them are over before they start. They cast a light on the future and make the person who originated them unforgettable. Anna has shed such a light on Siam."

No. 5

Is it who you know?

Vancouver philanthropist and my personal mentor Joe Segal (see Chapter 2) once said: "The statement 'it's not what you know, but who you know' is incorrect. If you don't know anything, you won't know anyone." Way to go, Joe!

No. 6

Catching on, but not up.

Mel Cooper, owner of independent radio stations CFAX 1070 and 107.8 FM in Victoria, British Columbia, competes every minute of every day with national chain radio stations that have deeper pockets than he does. But for more than 20 years, his AM station has been a consistent community leader.

Walk through the city centre of Victoria with Mel and you'll be constantly stopped by people who want to congratulate him on some aspect of the personal and corporate contribution he keeps making to his adopted city. In 1998 they made him an honorary citizen of Victoria for his years of giving and serving.

Mel says: "If we serve customers with creativity, competence and commitment, the competition may catch on, but they will never catch up."

No. 7

Cash flow is king.

How about this for a thought? Cash flow is more important than assets or net worth. Cash flow keeps a business going and growing. Assets are nothing more than numbers on a balance sheet.

No. 8

Sales make things happen.

If you are going to start your own business, you must understand the sales process. Nothing happens until somebody sells something. If sales don't keep happening, your company won't grow.

No. 9

Dare to be Positive

I recently read that men and women who have a history of being positive in their twenties, thirties, forties and fifties are not likely to have serious chronic diseases when they reach their sixties. At this writing I am 59. Other than being a bit overweight, I am in perfect "chronic" health.

Dare to be positive. You'll live longer.

No. 10

Be Enthusiastic

The word enthusiasm comes from the Greek word *entheos*, which means "God within." In most cases, the happiest and most interesting people are those who have found the secret of maintaining their enthusiasm—that God within.

My dad taught me the power of enthusiasm. He used to say: "I have never met an enthusiastic failure." My motivational guru Earl Nightingale said that the saddest days of our lives are those days in which we can find nothing to be enthusiastic about. You have to agree with him? The most fortunate people are those who keep energizing enthusiasm.

There are two keys to enthusiasm. The first comes from learning, and the second comes from accomplishment. Learning new things keeps our interest and enthusiasm high. The second key often ties into the first. It's hard to accomplish something new without first *learning* something new.

The most enthusiastic people are on top of life regardless of their status. As I keep saying, don't be the kind of person who brightens a room by leaving it. Enter the room to brighten it. Show off your confident, enthusiastic approach to life.

No. 11
Financial Freedom

George Siguardson is one of Canada's most successful insurance agents, and his list of achievements and awards is legendary. George lives in Winnipeg, and has sold at least 15 policies a month for the past 15 years. We recently met at a Canadian insurance conference where I was a guest speaker. George sent me a copy of his book, which among other pearls of wisdom, includes a fascinating piece on financial freedom.

George says that by the time you are 40, you will either be *earning* interest or *paying* interest. Whatever you are doing at 40, you will probably do for the rest of your life.

George's keys to financial freedom?

• No credit card debt.

• Taxes paid.

• Ownership of your own home.

• A maximized RRSP.

• At least 10 times your income in life insurance.

• Disability income coverage as high as 75 per cent of your earnings.

Only when these goals are achieved should you expand into other investments such as mutual funds, real estate, tax shelters or personal business interests. You may not agree with George, but his benchmarks are certainly worthy of serious consideration.

No. 12
You Never Know

His name was Fleming, and he was a poor Scottish farmer. One day, while trying to eke out a living for his family, he heard a cry for help coming from a nearby bog. He dropped his tools and ran. There, mired to his waist in mud, was a terrified boy, screaming and struggling to free himself. Farmer Fleming saved the lad from what could have been a slow and terrifying death.

The next day, a fancy carriage pulled up to the Scotsman's farm, and an elegantly dressed nobleman stepped out and introduced himself as the father of the boy Farmer Fleming had saved.

"I want to repay you," said the nobleman. "You saved

my son's life."

"No, I can't accept payment for what I did," the Scottish farmer said, and at that moment, the farmer's own son came to the door.

"Is that your son?" the nobleman asked.

"Yes," said the farmer.

"I'll make you a deal. Let me take him and give him a good education. If the lad is anything like his father, he'll grow to be a man you can be proud of."

And that he did. In time, Farmer Fleming's son graduated from St. Mary's Hospital Medical School in London, and went on to become Sir Alexander Fleming, the discoverer of penicillin.

Years afterward, the nobleman's son was stricken with pneumonia, and penicillin saved his life.

The name of the nobleman? Lord Randolph Churchill. His son? Winston Churchill.

Someone once said that what goes around comes around. Work like you don't need the money. Love like you've never been hurt. Dance as if no one is watching.

CHAPTER 14

Dare To Be Fat Free

GIVE OR TAKE, I've made about 1,500 speeches in the last 20 years. Those who have heard me on more than one occasion know that my best material is sometimes repeated. That's the way it is on any circuit of this kind.

Unlike television, where a performer's best material can be delivered to the whole country in a single stint, and is old hat as soon as it's out there, I speak to audiences one group at a time. And what happens is that until I'm hired to do my stuff for a PBS fundraiser, I can effectively use some of it more than once.

Like my exercise story.

Over the years, I haven't been big on exercise, and my body has reflected it well. I'll admit to being one of those short, round guys who often hides his shape and his tendency to portliness—is there such a word?—behind a bigger smile and a warmer handshake. Standing in front of any number of microphones in any number of cities, I have told audiences that my definition of a personal exercise program is to relax in a warm bath and fight the current when I pull the plug. Either in admiration or in sympathy, audiences invariably explode with laughter.

But lately things have changed for this Legge, and writing about it will hopefully guarantee that the momentum for goals of less weight and a better life will continue.

A while back, as I approached the age of 60, and dreamed of good things yet to come, I also came to the realization that if I were not in good health, those dreams could well become nightmares. If you're not up to physical scratch, there are lots of things that you just can't do—and I've worked long and hard to enjoy what I hope will be the fruits of my golden years, or any other color that's offered!

So I had a physical, and got myself a personal trainer. I don't go to *his* place. He comes to mine. Every morning at seven, Adrian Balodis, B.P.E., knocks on the front door and another sweaty session kick-starts my day.

I have all the stuff—a bike, a gruelling treadmill, a huge ball—and all of it is part of an hour of work that is turning this round little man into an entirely reborn specimen of physical perfection. Or so I keep telling myself.

But it's paying off. As it says on the cover of this book, Who Dares Wins. And if the SAS wants another recruit for one of its madcap maneuvers, I'm ready, guys!

My weight is down, and everything else that matters is up. It's happening, and all kidding aside, I feel much, much better than I did before.

So I could give some additional substance to this chapter, and perhaps make him famous at the same time, I asked Adrian if he could contribute some thoughts on all of this to the book, and he did.

This is more or less what he said:

With more than 30 billion fat cells in the average body, it's no wonder that most individuals who are trying to lose weight find the task so daunting—especially considering that each of these cells has the potential to increase in size up to a thousand times its original state!

Before we can attempt to change, it's best that we have a better understanding of why the fat is there.

Our bodies love fat! It is our survival in times of famine, and it appears that many of us are hunkering down for a long famine indeed. While there appears to be little risk of famine these days, our bodies respond to ancient commands. When we first stood upright 40,000 years ago, we became hunters and gatherers, and laying on fat in the good times took care of the times of lean.

Unfortunately, hunting these days takes place at buffet tables, and we stuff ourselves as if the threat of famine is right over the next horizon.

Understanding our body is one issue. Resisting food marketing in our always-changing society is another.

The term 'supersize' was unheard of until a few years ago, and now it dominates the way fast food outlets market their products. For ever-gullible consumers, supersize simply means adding more nutritionally empty fat and sugar calories. Considering that a large pop may contain as much as 72 ounces, which means 72 teaspoons of sugar, it is not surprising that North American obesity levels are hovering around 50 per cent!

It's scary to think where these obesity levels will go. With intakes approaching those of sumo wrestlers, combined with exercise expenditure rates bordering on inactive, it should come as no surprise that waistlines continue to expand.

Thankfully, the solution is, in theory, quite simple. Expend more calories than we intake! Do diets work in isolation from exercise? Obviously not. There's a new diet 'miracle' on bookstore shelves every week. And a Ph.D.'s theory, pumped by a celebrity's spectacular results, is no guarantee at all that it will work for you or me. In one survey of 29,000 weight loss strategies, fewer than six per cent were found to be effective and 13 per cent of them were plain dangerous!

Having worked as a personal trainer for 10 years, I tell my clients that if they truly want to lose weight, it's a mathematical issue that can be addressed through behavior modification.

The formula? If one pound of body fat equals 3,500 kcal, establishing a deficit of 500 kcal per day through a combination of increased activity and modified intake will lose you a pound of weight a week. That's it, the secret to weight loss.

It's a simple concept, but a difficult application. Why? Because it takes a great deal of hard work both physically and mentally to make it happen. And the truth is that not everyone is capable of this kind of radical change in a traditionally unhealthy lifestyle.

But if you *are* ready to change, throw out those apple cider vinegar pills, forget the latest fad diet, and don't even think about liposuction. In the long haul, none of these approaches is going to make a hill of beans—now *there's* a diet thought!—difference.

For weight loss success, consider these alternatives:

• Consume approximately six small meals a day, with fruits, vegetables and whole grains being the bulk of your intake. (Consult a registered dietitian for specific issues. Remember that anyone can claim to be a 'nutritionist.' Look for the credentials R.D. for credible nutritional information.)

• Start strengthening your muscles with weight training to increase your metabolism—which drops one per cent a year after age 30 and two per cent a year after age 40.

• Get into cardiovascular exercise five times a week. Build up to an hour in duration and keep the heart rate at about 65 per cent of its maximum rate.

• Keep a journal, and write down *everything* that you consume. Log all of your cardio activity.

So that's it. And even as I write, my pants are beginning to slip past my slender hips.

I think it's time for a nice hot bath.

CHAPTER 15

The Astronaut

I'VE NEVER BEEN MUCH of a weekend carpenter. It can be frustrating enough to rise to the challenge of a round of golf, and I shudder to think about how I might do with a saw—power or otherwise. My preference is to watch latter-day media heroes as they work their wonders in television workshops—and get it right every single time!

The only thing I remember about carpentry is what must

surely be its first law, which says: "Measure twice, cut once." The rule can save you a whole lot of messed up wood, and practised with consistency, it can perhaps give you the confidence to go onto greater workshop challenges. Like hammering nails, for instance.

I thought about this measure-twice-cut-once thing a year or so ago when I met Canadian astronaut Julie Payette, who came to Vancouver to speak at a St. John Ambulance event in which I too was participating.

Julie is a spectacular lady. Born in 1963 in Montreal, she is not only an astronaut, but she holds a multi-engine commercial pilot licence with instrument and float ratings. She plays piano, and has sung with the Montreal Symphonic Orchestra Chamber Choir, the Piacere Vocale in Basel, Switzerland, and with the Tafelmusik Baroque Orchestra Choir in Toronto. She is fluent in French and English, and is conversational in Spanish, Italian and Russian. She enjoys running, skiing, racquet sports and scuba diving. Her biography didn't mention carpentry, but I have complete confidence that she could probably whip up an armoire or two before breakfast.

Julie Payette flew on Space Shuttle Discovery in May-June 1999 as part of the crew of STS-96, a 10-day logistics and resupply mission to the International Space Station. She became the first Canadian to participate in an International Space Station assembly mission and to board the station.

When Julie spoke to the St. John Ambulance group, I took some notes, and among other things about which she spoke with such confidence, grace and eloquence, was the fact that in space no switch is flicked until the action is cleared not once, not twice, but *three* times by another crew member.

On earth in the workshop, it's measure twice, cut once.

In space, it's ask three times, and flick once.

On earth, families, businesses and any number of other organizations function more effectively when there is a degree of teamwork. In space, it is absolutely vital that the crew works as one.

Among many other things that she had to do in preparation for her space assignment, Julie Payette had to study and understand Russian to help turn a diverse collection of earth people into a single-minded, completely conversant space *team*.

"Now?"

"Nyet!"

In space, said Julie, it's not only vital to work as a team, but to work with a plan. On earth, we talk about plans, and sometimes we develop reasonably *good* plans, but if things go wrong, we can always try again. In space, you don't get second chances when big things go wrong. And you know what to do next because the plan is in place.

Would we do things better here on earth if we not only had a plan, but if we knew that we didn't have the option to keep on messing around with something until we got it right?

You can't call 911 in space. You can't open the window for more air. You can't say: "Hey, it didn't work. But don't worry, we'll get around to it next month."

Julie Payette told us that probably the greatest fault of all of us is that we delude ourselves into believing that we have great knowledge. The view from space is that we have so much more to learn about what she and other astronauts call "spaceship earth."

Astronauts, like none of the rest of us, get a very good view of the big earth picture. They see our blue oceans, our green forests, our snow-capped mountains and our deserts.

But they also see the things that have gone wrong, the horrible mistakes that have smudged our planet, maybe forever.

I kept my notes from Julie's presentation because ask three times and flick once makes a lot of sense to me.

Not just in space, but right here on spaceship earth.

CHAPTER 16

From Russia With 50 Ruples

SOME OF THE BEST IDEAS are sparked or are revealed over a good lunch, and an invitation to 'do lunch' is one that I rarely decline.

Back in about 1995, businessman, philanthropist, friend and mentor Joe Segal—you will read about him elsewhere in this book—invited me to join him for lunch at his favorite table at Chartwell in Vancouver's Four Seasons Hotel. And of course, I accepted.

Along with the great food that day, and all of the other wisdom that he invariably shares when we meet, I learned that Joe and other visionaries had come up with a plan to add a spectacular new dimension to the downtown Vancouver campus of Simon Fraser University. For those of you who are unfamiliar with the scene, the Lower Mainland of British Columbia has two major universities—the long-established University of British Columbia, and Simon Fraser University. SFU, as it is affectionately called, has two 'plants.' Its original spectacular building, designed by architect Arthur Erickson, is located atop a mountain in the Vancouver suburb of Burnaby. The university also serves its student complement at Harbour Centre, a high-rise in the heart of downtown Vancouver.

Right across the street from the downtown SFU campus is a temple-like building that since the early part of the last century had served as a bank. Like many structures that are more than about 10 minutes old in burgeoning Vancouver, its future existence, without some kind of dramatic intervention, may have been in doubt. But developer Peter Eng, who owned it, and was undertaking a major mixed-use project in the area, made a bold gesture and donated the building to the university. His reasons, he said, were a mix of philanthropy, enlightened self-interest and concrete commercial benefit. Whatever, it was a generous and much-appreciated gift.

So now Simon Fraser University had another building, and a challenge to make appropriate use of it. And I was hearing about all of this over lunch with Joe, who along with his other major credits, is also SFU Chancellor Emeritus and back then was a man obviously on a new and important mission.

I went back to the files of our magazine *BCBusiness* and found an article that Gerald Haslam wrote around that time to help me with the background on how the plan to revitalize this heritage treasure would come together. And in due course, I will introduce you to an individual who put up the seed money to make it happen, who dared and won—and helped to make a university's dream come true.

In ancient Rome, Haslam wrote, more than 100 citizens would debate the issues of the day seated in rising concentric circular rows in a room called the *comitium,* near the Senate. For Jack Blaney, SFU's then vice president for Harbour Centre and Continuing Studies, and the man who was researching ways to determine how best to make use of the new building, this detail from history was an "exciting" find.

SFU's first thought had been to use the building to expand traditional meeting space across the street from its Harbour Centre campus. But the more people Blaney and his colleagues talked to, the more research they did, the more they became convinced that the building should become a departure in meeting spaces, a unique venture, a step into both the past and future of discussion and decision-making, a place for what Blaney called "dialogue in the round."

The conference centre prospectus went on to say that dialogue is non-judgmental discourse . . . it seeks neither simple compromise nor compliance, but harmony through learning how to work and act together.

The university saw its new centre as being capable of hosting gatherings as diverse as academic conclaves and major events like gatherings of the Group of Seven.

The only big issue back in 1995 was money. Haslam's article said that construction costs would total $10 million—the building had good 'bones' but there would be much to do—plus a $5-million endowment fund to help offset operating costs. These numbers would escalate along the way.

Joe Segal, "because of my long-term association with the university and because I believe in the objectives of the international conference centre," would head up the fundraising team.

I won't go into the details of how the money all came together, but suffice to say that under Joe's arm-twisting leadership, the money was raised, and in September 2000, the Morris J. Wosk Centre for Dialogue was officially opened, and I was honored to be there.

Business in Vancouver, our principal business-news competitor, and one of the best of its kind in the business, published a commemorative booklet to mark the occasion, and also to honor Morris Wosk, whose donation of more than $3 million made the centre possible.

In his introduction, SFU Vice-President External Relations David Mitchell said: "Among all of the friends who assisted with this project, one person stands out as first among equals: Morris J. Wosk. His early and significant support for this project helped provide the leverage that was necessary to translate the vision into a *fait accompli.*

"Morris J. Wosk's personal story . . . is one of a self-made man who has generously contributed to our community in numerous untold ways . . . The conference centre that bears his name is without parallel, a meeting place that will truly make a difference."

While I don't plan to go into the architectural details—please come for a visit when next you're in Vancouver!—I *would* like to tell you about some of the highlights of Morris Wosk's inspirational life that were collected by *Business in Vancouver* and included in the commemorative program. I have obtained permission to freely glean from the magazine's fine copy.

Morris Wosk lives in an apartment high above Vancouver's English Bay. He was born in Odessa on July 4, 1917, a time of great social upheaval, when his family was shaken often by fear, pogroms and Cossack gangs.

Despite the toughest of times, the Wosk family was luckier than most. His great-grandfather had served for 25 years in the imperial army, granting him a parcel of land when he left. He became one of a handful of Jewish landowners at a time when Jews were barred from universities and forced to practice their religion in secret.

The article went on: "Eventually, the Wosk land was passed down through the family to Joseph, Morris Wosk's father. But even as landowners, the family never felt secure. One day, Morris recalls, the Cossacks arrived and began searching the area for Jewish families. Morris's parents disguised themselves as peasant farmers and the children—Morris and his brother—were hidden in a cart and covered with hay. Morris remembers the Cossacks' yells becoming louder as they thrust their swords through the hay above him."

In fear for their lives, Morris's parents began making plans to leave the country and in August 1928 they left for Canada, arriving in Vancouver three months later.

"On the train trip across Canada, we felt like citizens of the world," says Morris. "I knew I wouldn't have to look over my shoulder anymore."

While Morris had problems learning a new language in Vancouver, he won friends by becoming their baseball hero. Much older than the kids in his class, every hit was a home run.

When he was 13, he raised cash by buying pots and pans at auction sales, cleaning them up and re-auctioning them for a tidy profit. Subsequently the family bought a horse and wagon and went into full-time peddling.

At 15, Morris and his older brother rented a store on downtown Granville Street. On opening day, the only stock they had on hand was an oak table and a radio. Their first sale was the radio.

They built up their stock with acquisitions from auctions and estate sales, replaced the horse and wagon with a pickup truck. They branched out into second-hand appliances and later into new goods, winning dealership favor by handling the big brands.

Morris became known as "Car Load Morry" because that's the way he bought appliances from manufacturers. By 1960, Wosk's Ltd. had 12 Lower Mainland outlets, and their slogan was "Nobody But Nobody Undersells Wosk."

Up front there were furniture and appliances. Paralleling that was a construction company building houses, apartments and hotels. The Blue Horizon Hotel, which opened in 1967, was the tallest building in Vancouver.

Morris told *Business in Vancouver* that he has never bought, sold, built or traded anything outside of Vancouver.

"Vancouver's my city and the sweetness of success is very great when I go for a drive on Sunday and see what I've accomplished. It gives me a great deal of pride."

Morris Wosk has donated more than $50 million to charitable causes, including the project that bears his name at SFU.

"My father told me, 'If you make 10 cents, put one cent

away, give one cent to charity and spend the rest, if you have to.' I know what it is to be poor and living in fear. It's something I will never forget."

Of his major donation to SFU, Morris said: "President Jack Blaney and Joseph Segal came to me with their plans for the Centre for Dialogue and said they were working hard to start the ball rolling on financing the project. I think I surprised them by writing a cheque there and then.

"Then I phoned the bank manager and said, 'Do you have enough money to cover the cheque?'

"Of all the buildings that I built, bought and sold, I am most proud of being associated with SFU's Dialogue Centre . . . There wouldn't be so many problems in the world if people were able to communicate with each other more effectively. I think that's what the centre is all about."

Morris Wosk's son, Rabbi Yosef Wosk, is director of Interdisciplinary Studies at SFU, and was recently named by the *Vancouver Sun* as one of British Columbia's top 10 thinkers. Yosef founded B.C.'s "remarkably successful Philosophers' Café series, in which the public gathers in restaurants and bistros to dig into a wide range of philo-sophical and social questions.

"At hundreds of Philosophers' Cafes, tens of thousands of British Columbians have had the opportunity, as Wosk says, to escape from stress and the electronic media and explore some of life's important questions over salad, cof-fee and wine. And, best yet, there's no test at the end."

When the Wosk Centre was opened, it was Yosef Wosk who delivered the celebratory addresses. He stepped in because shortly before, Morris Wosk's wife Dena—to whom he had been married for 54 years—had passed away.

The addresses in morning and evening ceremonies, included these words:

"Combined with the historic architecture [of the building] is cutting-edge technology. And yet they work together, the old and the new, the vision and the reality. Here government will speak with the people; business will interface with pedagogues; scholars will sit as equals with the unlearned so that in the midst of dialogue a deeper appreciation might emerge. Here there will be opportunities . . . to join head to heart and thought to action. This, too, is dialogue.

"This Centre for Dialogue marks the significant expansion of our downtown campus, here in the heart of the city, this centre in the round, this graceful cathedral dedicated to dialogue, so that we may learn to listen, to hear, to appreciate one another.

"To cultivate the ability to listen deeply is one of the sacred roots of my tradition: *Shema Yisrael . . .* These were among the final words that my wife, Dena, *aleha ha'shalom,* heard just moments before she passed away two weeks ago. Those ancient words encouraging us to listen, will continue to reverberate here in the midst of these noble circular chambers. And so it will come to pass that whenever people of good will gather here, they will be inspired by Heaven and supported by the good Earth.

"We all dream, but most dreams are absorbed into the darkness of sleep's dark embrace. Few are those who remember their dreams and rarer still are those who can interpret them. Only one in 10,000, however, stand as we do today, in the midst of a dream come true. From inspiration to interpretation, how fortunate we are to witness what to others, one day, will be legend. We live in extraordinary times: this building and its mission are extraordinary, indeed.

"I have been nourished by my beliefs, and have pursued balanced harmony whenever possible. I have embraced courage and followed my dreams while always respecting the memories of our elders, our history, and our heritage. I have learned to be strict but only when necessary; to expect high standards from myself as well as from others. I have also been known to melt in tears at deeply emotional moments. Anger or disappointment is rare: those who know me can attest that it is humor and a good laugh with friends that I value most of all.

"What I've learned I have put into action, for it is not enough to only have thoughts, lofty as they may be, nor is it enough to merely talk about our ideas, eloquent as those words may sound. It is imperative that we also translate our best intentions into deeds for everyone's benefit.

"One thousand years ago the Hebrew Sage, Rashi,

remarked: 'Naked a man comes into the world, and naked he leaves it. After all his toil he carries away nothing— except appreciation for the deeds that he has left behind.'

"On reflection, I think that it is better to give from the heart while the heart is still beating. Following this philosophy has given me even more than I have given to others. It reminds me of Sir Winston Churchill's observation: 'We make a living by what we get. But we make a life by what we give.'

" . . . I am truly overwhelmed to have had the opportunity to be a part of this magnificent project. I am grateful to the Almighty for giving me the ability to provide for my family and for giving me the wisdom and the will to support our health, educational and cultural institutions as well as individuals in need.

"With a heart torn by tears, and a mind preoccupied with married memories, I pledge my continuing support and dedication to a constructive and creative life for our community. On behalf of my entire family, I sincerely wish our university the very best as she continues on her path to greatness, on her journey from strength to strength.

"May we all be blessed with wisdom, inspiration and good health so that together we can carry on this Great Dialogue of Life."

These words were spoken at the building's invocation during the lighting of the Havdalah candle:

Blessed is the match that is consumed in kindling flame,
Blessed is the flame that dances in the dark to enlighten
life eternal.
Blessed is the life consumed in the care for others,
And in the lifelong search for meaning
That we may receive the teachings of ancient ages
And discover the secrets of tomorrow's dawn.

Over the years Morris has been honored at many Testimonial Dinners and received numerous awards for his exemplary leadership, effort, initiative and support. He was awarded an Honorary Doctorate of Philosophy by the Hebrew University in 1989 and an Honorary Doctorate of Laws from Simon Fraser University in 1996. In 1990 he received a Gold Medal from the State of Israel Bonds, and in 1996 he was amongst a select group of only 25 individuals worldwide honored with the Jerusalem 3000 Award for his long-standing and continuing support of Israel.

In 1992 Mr. Wosk was appointed a Member of the Order of Canada and in 1994 he was honored by the province when he was appointed to the Order of British Columbia. In 1996 he was awarded the Freedom of the City of Vancouver and was presented with a Key to the City of Jerusalem.

It seems like yesterday that I had that memorable lunch with Joe. I'm glad I said yes to his invitation.

CHAPTER 17

The "Real" Great One

IT IS RARE, *very* rare, that I ever worry about standing up in front of an audience. Give me a crowd of 10, a hundred, a hundred thousand, or a television audience of a hundred million, and I'm pumped and ready to go.

If *you're* not nervous, *I'm* not nervous. You're ready to *receive*, and I'm prepared and ready to *give*. Lead me to the mike!

I know there are people who would rather die than present themselves to an audience. It's a predicament worse than anything they could imagine. And I feel genuinely sorry for them, even if I can't understand their predicament.

Me? An audience for me is a tonic, a shot in the arm, an elixir of extraordinary proportion.

Waiting in the Green Room, hearing the introduction, the adrenaline starts to fill all of my corners, and no matter *what* the venue, it's a rush.

Except on one occasion in Miami, Florida.

On that day, before I began, I had to confront and lay low the ghost of The Great One.

Before Gretzky was the Great One, there was the Great One Gleason. Jackie Gleason. A brilliant, funny man, who I had worshipped all my life as the kind of brilliant, funny man that *I* would like to be.

If you're too young to know a lot about Jackie Gleason, catch him sometime in one of the reruns of *The Honeymooners*. I have no doubt they'll keep playing the series forever. Watch his face, his body, and the nuances of his timing. Listen to the highs and lows of his language, his ability to drag you in and spit you out. If you have trouble with his character, bus driver Ralph Kramden, appreciate Gleason's ability to *portray* Ralph—doing it all in front a live audience in Miami Beach, Florida.

Jackie, according to my research, moved from New York to Miami Beach in the early '60s. The word was that being the keenest of golfers, he wanted more sunshine in his life than New York could offer, and California seemed like a good place to go.

But others, seeing great PR opportunity if he were to arrive in the neighborhood, made an offer from Miami that he couldn't refuse. It included a home right on the fairway of the Miami Beach Country Club. One of his perks included "a private golf cart built like a miniature Rolls-Royce. It had radio, television and turn signals. It also was kept well stocked with chilled Dom Perignon, scotch, vodka, gin, olives, mixers, and all the other accoutrements of a rolling Toots Shor's."

For five years, the show proclaimed itself as originating "from the sun and fun capital of the world." It opened every time with a glamor shot of the Miami Beach shoreline—and the city was delighted with all of the publicity.

The show too was a huge success, and on Saturday nights until 1971, we would all tune in to watch The Great One, to hear him say: "How sweet it is!" "A little travelling music please." "Awa-a-a-ay we go!" We loved the June Taylor Dancers from every angle, his characters Reggie, Joe, the Poor Soul, Charley the Loudmouth, Pedro the Mexican, Stanley R. Sogg, and many others. It was a show exactly right for the times. And for me, Mr. Gleason was indeed The Great One.

It was in the Miami Beach Auditorium that Jackie used to do his shows, and it is the same auditorium that today is the Jackie Gleason Theater of the Performing Arts.

Dating back to 1950, the auditorium has been home to the biggest and best. Frank Sinatra, Bob Hope and Jack Benny were there. Tapings of the *Dick Clark Show* and the *Ed Sullivan Show* happened, along with the Miss Universe and Miss USA pageants. Horowitz played there, and so did Itzak Perlman. Tony Bennett and Liza Minnelli were there, and in later years, so was *Phantom of the Opera* and *Riverdance.*

But most of all Jackie Gleason was there, and on that stage where he had performed, I had been contracted to speak—with the ghost of The Great One watching over me.

Scheduled for an 8:30 a.m. start, I was in the theatre (excuse my Canadian spelling!) at 7:20, 10 minutes ahead of a scheduled 7:30 sound check.

"Check. Check. Check."

I had done 90-minute 'keynotes' hundreds of times before and now I had sweaty palms and shaking legs!

I wasn't worried about Mickey Rooney, Rex Harrison, the Gypsy Kings and all of the others. All I could think about was this giant of a man saying: "Awa-a-a-a-ay we go!"

Jamie McDonough, the show's director, assigned me to "Star Dressing Room D." Just 15 feet from stage right, it was less than 100 feet from the famed rehearsal hall that I noted came complete with mirrors and ballet bars. I thought for a moment about the June Taylor Dancers. I was 30 feet from the flattering pink Green Room.

While much of the theatre has been refurbished over the years, one area that has been left as it was is a specially constructed two-bedroom apartment upstairs that was built for the exclusive use of The Great One.

Manny Fernandez, a Cuban refugee who was in charge of daily affairs at the theatre, said that the apartment was off limits to folks like me, and I respected the rule. At the time, I had no doubt at all that had I gone in there, the ghost of Jackie would have greeted me at the door with a gigantic: "Awa-a-a-a-ay we go!"

When you're really nervous about doing something, your knees *do* actually knock. And your mouth dries up, and your eyes don't function the way they should, and the hair stands up on the back of your neck.

Some say that to deliver a great performance, a degree of nervousness is important. It heightens the senses, raises the bar. I had never before felt that bar raising was important to *my* performance. I just go on, and let the audience give me the vibes I need to make things happen.

Was Jackie Gleason nervous going before a live nationwide audience every Saturday night? I have no idea, but I suspect that anyone who kept saying, "how sweet it is!" was probably as loose as he looked.

With minutes to go that morning, I confronted all of these unfamiliar fears I was having, and instead of being intimidated by this favorite giant of my past, I decided to draw on his great strength, on the likelihood that if he was actually sitting in the front row that morning, he would be the most supportive person there.

I got strength not just from thinking that, but from the good things I was beginning to feel about how privileged I was to be starring on Jackie Gleason's very own stage.

I said to myself that if I allow fear to control me, I can't possibly perform to my own expectations. I really had no choice but to push all of that negative stuff away—to go out there big, to dare and win.

Jackie loved golf. But as I well know, no matter how much they load up your cart with fancy extras, it still comes with a governor that controls its stately speed. That morning, what I had to do was override my own governor, move out of low gear and on into the kind of heady front-of-audience happiness that I knew and remembered so well.

Warm, familiar feelings returned, and I saw images of that rubbery old Gleason face filling an ancient black and white screen.

"Ladies and gentlemen. From Vancouver, British Columbia, will you please give a Miami Beach sunshine welcome to our keynote speaker . . . Peter Legge."

To ringing applause from 2,700 people, I walked with confidence to the microphone.

How sweet it was!

CHAPTER 18

Fore — Charity

I NEVER KNEW WHETHER OR NOT a golf tournament that had
my name on it would be successful or not. You take a
chance on things like this, and I knew from the start that the
Legge name didn't have quite the ring in the golf world that
other names did. Bob Hope? No problem. Peter Legge?
Possible problem.

But in the summer of 1995, I wanted to do something

good for the Canadian Red Cross, and figured that a round of golf on a great course, backed by some fabulous sponsors, might just work. And what the heck, the Peter Legge Charity Golf Classic had a nice ring to it!

Choosing as our venue the Furry Creek Golf and Country Club, crafted on a challenging mountainside halfway between Vancouver and the resort town of Whistler, B.C., we went to work with a will to win.

At the end of the day, and what a day it was, we had raised $22,000. By international standards it wasn't a fortune, but it was good enough to drive us into a second year, when the cheque to the Red Cross was $25,000.

We went back to Furry Creek for a third year and the day netted $32,000, and $31,000 the year after that.

In 1999, we decided to share the wealth among four new worthy organizations—the National Advertising Benevolent Society, the BC Paraplegic Association, St. John Ambulance, and the Royal Westminster Regiment Volunteer Band. The take for the day jumped to $47,500 as more and more sponsors and players got on board to be involved in our program.

On July 17, 2000, the event raised more than $49,000, and we'll keep on going.

The event in 2000 was quite spectacular. One hundred and sixty golfers in a sold-out day. Armed sentries from the Royal Westminster Regiment guarded the clubhouse doors and St. John Ambulance cadets saluted players as they entered. The 24-piece Royal Westminster Volunteer Band played throughout the morning and their fanfare trumpeters signaled the shotgun start. It was a sound that rang loud and clear through the coastal mountains, echoed off the walls of beautiful Howe Sound, and the rocks and fairways of Furry Creek!

If you want to play next year, please give me a call at 604-299-7311 or e-mail plegge@canadawide.com.

Who dares wins, say I. But Furry Creek will give you a run for your money!

CHAPTER 19

A Lesson In Leadership

ON JANUARY 15, 1942, the day after I was born, General George Patton arrived at Indio, California, to take command of a desert training centre.

Except for a few friends, relatives and others who showed up to congratulate my mum, and study me through a nursery window, my birth, at a hospital in England, went largely unheralded. I came into the world with a gentle squawk. Patton came into town in a sirens-screaming motorcade.

Waiting expectantly for a traditional motivating speech, Patton's officers and men watched him dismount from his car at 11 a.m., the precise minute he was scheduled to take command. He saluted the troops and said: "I assume command of the First Armored Corps. At ease!"

There was no "glad to be with you," no "happy to be aboard," no "we'll make a great team." Patton simply said: "We are at war with a tough enemy. We must train millions of men to be soldiers! We must make them tough in mind and in body. Every man in this command will be able to run a mile in 15 minutes with a full military pack, including a rifle. We will start running from this point in exactly 30 minutes! I will lead!"

For Patton, leadership meant being in command. That's the way he saw it—being in command. A leader leads. Period.

I have read that good leaders inspire people to have confidence in their leadership. Great leaders also inspire people to have confidence in themselves. I never met General George Patton, but I would guess that while there may have been muttering in the ranks from time to time, and amazement and even disgust at his manner and style, when it came to the crunch, his troops had confidence not only in his leadership, but in themselves.

If you plan to lead, you can't sit around waiting for

something to happen and you can't always be Mr. or Ms. Nice Person. Leadership is never given, leadership is taken. Leaders make bold moves. Leaders take risks. Leaders make use of their own ingenuity to do what they have to do. Everyone, including the best leaders, will make mistakes, but all of us will savor the victories we will win over great negative odds. Amateurs built the ark. Professionals built the *Titanic*. The Ark survived the flood. *Titanic* hit an iceberg and went to the bottom.

Thousands of books have been written on the subject of leadership, and for inspiration and guidance, I lap these books up with great regularity. My own library includes inspirational works by John Maxwell, Stephen Covey, Brian Tracy, Denis Waitley, Nido Qubein, Max DePree, Ken Blanchard, John Gardner, and many others. More will emerge in the future.

For 25 years I have led Canada Wide Magazines through good times and bad. Challenges have included three recessions, a 150-per-cent increase in the price of paper, and an ever-changing business climate. The positives? We are debt free, we have a staff of 100-plus great people who produce 20 magazines with annual sales of more than $25 million.

How did we do it? What leadership skills did I use to propel Canada Wide forward? I can't say that I rolled into town like George Patton did, but in my own way, I have likely patterned myself after Patton, and many others who have shared their leadership secrets.

Canada Wide Magazines is the Number One magazine publisher in Western Canada, and for 25 years, these are the seven basic leadership principles I have employed to assure the company's success.

Leadership Law No. 1

Sometimes being a leader means pissing people off. You can't marry all the girls, and you can't give your employees everything they want. Businesses thrive when tough calls are made, and leaders have to make tough calls. Leadership can be a lonely, often distasteful job, but once the choice has been made, the job has to be done. Leaders have to lead. Period.

According to Sir Adrian Cadbury, being able to make unpopular decisions is a key aspect of ethical leadership. Cadbury is head of Cadbury Schweppes PLC, one of the world's largest food and beverage companies.

Sir Adrian said: "The company that takes drastic action in order to survive is more likely to be criticized publicly than the one which fails to grasp the nettle and gradually declines. There is always a temptation to postpone difficult decisions, but it is not in society's best interest that hard choices should be avoided because of public clamor."

Good leaders won't always win popularity contests, with their own employees or with the public. On the other hand, they *will* win favor with their shareholders. And in business, that's the way it is.

Leadership Law No. 2

Stay focused on the Big Picture. Read and reread your Mission Statement.

Canada Wide Magazines' Mission Statement is outlined in full in Chapter 1, but so you won't have to flip back, here again are the values that guide us:

Honesty and integrity in all of our dealings, both inside Canada Wide and outside the company, are cornerstones of our business.

We are committed to encouraging, developing and maintaining the highest levels of professional expertise in every employee to ensure excellence in all aspects of the products and services we provide.

We are committed to keeping our eyes trained on the future and to encourage the sharing of new ideas among all of our employees.

We are committed to thoughtful planning and responsive management in all sectors of the company to ensure the company's ongoing financial success.

We are committed to developing a thorough understanding of the unique needs of every client and to developing and delivering top-quality products that fully meet those needs.

We are committed to the growth and development of all of our employees and to ensuring their success and future within Canada Wide.

We are committed to supporting charitable endeavors

and to putting our resources to work for the betterment of the community.

Stephen Covey, the renowned author and consultant, believes that one reason it's difficult for today's businesspeople to stay focused is that we waste our energy on "urgent and or unimportant" events. We do this, he says, because anything that is urgent tends to "seem" important.

Phone calls, e-mails, faxes, pagers, interruptions—all of these create a sense of urgency, no matter how unimportant their content may be. Think about it.

In the Jewish tradition there is a holiday—Simchat Torah—that celebrates the completion of the cycle of one full reading of the Torah—the Five Books of Moses. When the readers finish, they roll the scroll all the way back to the beginning and start again. By continually reading the Torah they stay in touch with the original core ideas they value.

Canada Wide doesn't own a restaurant, or a pub, or a newspaper. We have stuck to our knitting by rereading our Mission Statement and becoming experts in the magazine publishing field in Western Canada.

Take your own company Mission Statement and its core values, and reread it at least once a month. My own company's Mission Statement and its core values are proudly displayed in our front lobby.

Leadership Law No. 3

Leaders are readers. It has been said that lifelong learning is the great equalizer. Exceptional leaders thrive by continuously developing themselves.

Peter Drucker, author of "Post Capitalist Society," said that a leader's role is to teach everyone in the organization to be devoted to his or her work. The leader must first lead. All employees have to see themselves as executives. You can't take anybody any further than you have been yourself.

Readers are not necessarily leaders but leaders are almost always readers. The person who is paving the way or setting the pace can wear out or dry up mentally as well as physically because the mind needs food.

Ask yourself these two questions. What have I learned in the last year to increase my bottom line performance? What do I plan to learn in the next year to further improve my bottom line performance?

Leadership Law No. 4

Leaders are Visionaries. One of the Proverbs of the Old Testament says that where there is no vision people perish. In business, in everything, there must be vision.

H.G. Wells, reflecting on how every human being can determine whether he or she has really succeeded in life, said that the true measure of success is the difference between what we made of ourselves, and what we *might* have made of ourselves.

Correct me if I'm wrong, but I maintain that you are a

better, more capable person than you have demonstrated so far, and I challenge you to start a crusade in your life—to dare to be your best. Think of the possibilities!

The only reason you are not the person you should be is that you don't dare to be that person. Once you dare, once you stop drifting with the crowd and face life courageously, life takes on a new significance, and new forces take shape within you.

"I have no fear of the future. Let us go forward into its mysteries. Let us tear aside the veils which hide it from our eyes and let us move onward with confidence and courage."

Leadership has a great deal to do with the future. This is largely because most of us live out, in practical terms, what we believe the future will be. When men and women see their future as one of promise and fruitfulness, they start living lives that are fuller, richer. They take the risks necessary for success.

On a corporate note, I believe we are in the golden age of magazines, and I have the vision and goal to be the very best of publishers. I remember the slogan of a Vancouver car dealership that said: "Not best because we're biggest, but biggest because we're best." Great thought!

Throughout history, great leaders have demonstrated that a gripping vision of the future is at the very heart of exceptional leadership. In the early 1940s, in the heat of the Second World War, a poster of Winston Churchill was plastered all over England. The bold words accompanying

Churchill's image simply said "Deserve Victory." It was integral to his life philosophy, and a nation was inspired.

"What is the use of living if not to strive for noble causes and to make this muddled world a better place to live in after we are gone."

Leadership Law No. 5

Good Leaders Plan Ahead. One great need in our world is for more sober, profitable thinking. Too often, people go about their business in a headlong way, never pausing to think of the potential results. A great mathematician said that if he had but three minutes to work at a problem on which his life depended, he would spend two of those minutes considering the best way to approach it. If you have a garden, the planning must come before the planting. It makes much more sense to work it all out with a pencil than it does with a shovel. Carefully plan ahead. Success in all things needs preparation. Equally important is the way in which we need to deal with others.

*Don't Say It

If you think that you are better

Than your neighbour 'cross the way,

Or that nature has endowed you

With a more perfect form of clay,

Don't say it.

If you know that you have talent,
And your neighbour naught but gold,
Or that all his goods are mortgaged
If the truth were only told,
Don't say it.

If you know some dreadful scandal,
Such as gossips always court,
And could add a few words to it
When they call for your support,
Don't do it.

Let your life be true and earnest,
Court discretion for your friend,
And though often you are tempted
A word to say that would offend,
Don't say it.

*The crimes of the tongue are evil words of unkindness, of anger, of malice, of envy, of bitterness, of harsh criticism, gossip, lying and scandal.

—*W.G. Jordan*

"Whoever determinedly sets about a business has half accomplished it. Your motto must be, 'Forward Now!' Do instantly whatever is to be done, and take the hours of recreation after business, never before it. When a regiment is under march, the rear is often thrown into confusion because the front does not move steadily and without interruption. It is the same with business. If that which is first in hand is not instantly, steadily and regularly dispatched other things accumulate behind, till affairs begin to press all at once, and no human brain can stand the confusion. Be, then, in the habit of punctuality and order. Always have an object in view. Let all your things have their place, and let each part of your business have its time."

—Sir Walter Scott, counsel to a young friend

Nothing in the world can take the place of persistence. Talent will not; nothing is more common than unsuccessful men with talent. Genius will not; unrewarded genius is almost a proverb. Education will not; the world is full of educated derelicts.

—Calvin Coolidge

You need Persistence, Patience and Push. The bulldog's claim to fame is based on a single great quality—he can hang on. Those little words, try, and begin, are sometimes great in their results. "I can't" never accomplished anything. "I will try" has achieved wonders.

Success comes to those who set goals
    And pursue them
    Regardless of obstacles and disappointments.

—Napoleon Hill

Leadership Law No. 6

Leaders pay a price to be successful. Great leaders pay a price to stay. What qualities, habits, disciplines got you where you are today? What leadership skills did you employ and what price did you pay to be successful? Don't forget that we never really arrive. Life is a continual process of development, but great leaders pay the price to stay.

Zig Ziglar once said: "Be a meaningful specific. Most people are meaningless generalities. Remember what got you there and keep daring to build on those qualities so you can stay on top."

Leadership Law No. 7

Positive attitude is everything. It was W. Clement Stone who coined the phrase PMA—Positive Mental Attitude. He also coined the phrase NMA—Negative Mental Attitude. He said: "I can't absolutely guarantee you will be successful with a positive mental attitude. But I can guarantee you won't be with a negative mental attitude."

Dr. Stanley, who wrote the best-selling book, "A Millionaire's Mind," interviewed a thousand millionaires and discovered that a whopping 62 per cent of those he interviewed claimed that the ability to get along with other men and women was the single most important quality they attributed to their enormous success.

It costs in the relationship you have with your spouse, your children, your neighbors, your community—and it most definitely costs in the relationship you have with people in your business.

As I get older I pay less attention to what men and women say but I pay attention to what they do.

I am not sure who said this, but I certainly believe it: "You can get everything you want in your life if you help enough other people get what they want in *their* lives."

People want to do business with people they like and respect. Ask yourself these questions: Who do you want to do business with? Are you the kind of person who brightens a room by leaving it? Are you the kind of person who is excited about life, has a rich, powerful, positive attitude and exudes that attitude every day in every situation?

Helen Keller once said, "If life is not an adventure, life is nothing." I say if life is not lived with a positive attitude, life is nothing. Dare to have a positive attitude and your wildest dreams are possible.

Never give in!
Never, never, never, never
In nothing great or small
Large or petty
Never give in except to convictions of honour and good sense.

— Sir Winston Churchill
October 29, 1941
Speech at the Harrow School

CHAPTER 20

The Speakers Roundtable

NAOMI RHODE IS CONSIDERED one of the finest speakers in North America. When she was president of the National Speakers Association, consisting of over 4,000 professional speakers, she selected as her theme for her year as President "The Privilege of the Platform." Having given over 1,500 speeches myself, I am very aware of the unique privilege it is to address any size audience anywhere. Oh yes, sometimes the travel—getting on and off planes, strange hotels, less than pleasant taxi drivers, sound systems that don't work, missing luggage—can be very taxing and stressful. When you are introduced to your audience the true professional is ready and pumped to entertain, educate, motivate and teach because it is a privilege to be a speaker.

The Greek physician Hippocrates, who died in 376 BC, once said, "The life so short . . . the craft so long to learn."

After almost 20 years in this business and a string of speaking awards denied most speakers, one Saturday morning at home my phone rang and it was the legendary Naomi Rhode on the other end inviting me to be a member of the very exclusive and prestigious Speakers Roundtable—an organization of only 20 of the very best speakers in the world.

Would I like to be a member? The only Canadian ever to be invited. How long does it take to say yes?

Not only the privilege of the platform but a privilege to be among the finest speakers in the world. At the end of this chapter I have listed who they are and where you can contact them.

I asked two members of the Speakers Roundtable, Nido Qubein, CSP, CPAE, and Danny Cox, CSP, CPAE, to contribute to this work. They readily accepted and the next two short chapters are used with their permission.

All 20 of the Speakers Roundtable dared to get on a platform and dared to be great. They all knew and still know what a privilege it is.

Speakers Roundtable Members

Dr. Tony Alessandra, PhD, CSP, CPAE

Ty Boyd, CSP, CPAE

Jim Cathcart, CSP, CPAE

Danny Cox, CSP, CPAE

Patricia Fripp, CSP, CPAE

William H. Gove, CSP, CPAE Emeritus

Art Holst, CPAE Emeritus

Charlie Jones, CPAE

Charlie Plumb

Nido Qubein, CSP, CPAE

Naomi Rhode, CSP, CPAE

Mark Sanborn, CSP, CPAE

Brian Tracy, CPAE

Dr. Herb True, CPAE Emeritus

Jim Tunney, EdD, CSP, CPAE

Thom Winninger, CSP, CPAE

Roger Crawford, CPAE

Don Hutson, CSP, CPAE

Scott McKain, CSP, CPAE

Bert Decker, CSP, CPAE

Dianna Booher, CSP

Peter Legge, CSP, CPAE

For more information contact:

Linda Hightower, Executive Director

Speakers Roundtable

Tel: (901) 767-0000

CHAPTER 21

Fear vs. Courage: It's Your Choice

By Danny Cox

from Chapter 36 of "There Are No Limits" (Career Press 1998)

"ONCE WHEN MARSHALL NEY was going to battle, looking down at his knees which were smiting together, he said, 'You may well shake; you would shake worse yet if you knew where I am going to take you.' Napoleon was so much impressed with the courage and resources of Marshall Ney, that he said, 'I have two hundred millions in my coffers, and I would give them all for Ney.' " —Orison Swett Marden.

What or who builds self-imposed barriers? A stone-mason named Fear, one who is highly skilled in building powerful barriers from nonexistent stones. Where does this craftsman live? In our minds. He's always there, but it's up to us whether he lives in the back of our minds or the front of our minds. Fear is the sworn enemy of adventure, which is the third and perhaps most exhilarating force driving no-limits achievement. And Fear goes exactly where we tell him to go.

We move fear from the back of our minds to the front of our minds by shifting our concentration away from our own courage, and choosing instead to focus on that which frightens us. Not only does that action change Fear's location but through the process of concentration, it means we actually start to strengthen Fear. Fear has no strength of its own; its only strength is that which we choose to give it.

When Fear defeats us, it does so because of our own mental focus. And unfortunately, the strength we pass along to Fear is the very strength we need to overcome it! If, on the other hand, we choose to push our goals, wrapped in courage, to the forefront of our minds, then barriers break. You already possess sufficient courage to initiate this process and see your personal adventure through. A person may not be born with an overabundance of talent, but he or she will certainly possess all the courage needed, whether used or unused, to develop the talent that is there. Long after passing on to the next world, we will be remembered by family and friends, not necessarily for our inborn talents, but for the amount of courage we used, especially during our times of trial. The strength and vividness of the memories our loved ones and friends hold of us after we are gone will be directly proportional to the amount of courage we have chosen to use.

Immediate Action: Starve your fear! Feed your courage! Embrace your adventure!

Point to ponder before you go on: "Fear knocked at the door. Faith answered. No one was there." (From above the fireplace at Hinds' Head Hotel, near London.)

CHAPTER 22

The Three Steps to Building A Winner's Attitude

From "How to Get Anything You Want" by Nido Qubein

THERE ARE THREE BASIC STEPS to developing a winner's attitude. They are simple to say and easy to understand, but they require more effort than anything you have ever tried.

STEP 1

Make a Strong and Permanent Commitment to Invest Your Life and Talents Only in Those Pursuits That Deserve Your Best Efforts!

If it's worth doing at all, it's worth doing to the best of your ability. If it's not worth the best you can do, it's not worthy of the winner's time.

Since I am often billed as an inspirational business speaker, I do try to motivate people by sharing things that I have learned from some of the most outstanding winners in history. But I'll let you in on a little secret: Nobody can really motivate another person. That is something that people can do only for themselves!

Anything less than that which calls forth the very best within you will not be important enough to motivate you to overcome all the obstacles that keep you from becoming a winner. When a goal matters enough to a person, that person will find a way—the resources—to accomplish what at first seemed impossible. For example, Alcoholics Anonymous has been highly successful at helping people overcome a most severe habit. Yet, any member of that fine organization will tell you that he or she can do nothing to help an alcoholic—until that person is totally committed to the goal of sobriety.

Only when you are totally committed to an overriding purpose will you put forth the effort required to overcome discouragement, misunderstanding from other people, and defeat. Consider the bumpy career of Abraham Lincoln. He:

Lost his job in 1832

Was defeated for the legislature in 1832

Failed in business in 1833

Was elected to legislature in 1834

Lost his sweetheart to death in 1835

Had a nervous breakdown in 1836

Was defeated for Speaker in 1838

Was defeated in bid for Congress in 1843

Was elected to Congress in 1846

Lost nominated bid for Congress in 1848

Was rejected for Land Officer in 1849

Was defeated for Senate in 1854

Lost nomination for Vice Presidency in 1856

Was again defeated for Senate in 1858

Was elected President in 1860

Only Lincoln's deep conviction that God had given him a mission to fulfill kept him going when most people would have quit. Such motivation might well be ridiculed in this day of glorification of the self—as it was in his day—but it contains the kind of stuff that causes people to become winners.

Of course, people with the winner's attitude know that fame and fortune are not the only measures of success. Public recognition and money are only the superficial ways of keeping score. What drives the winners to put forth Her-culean effort, to bounce back from failures and defeats, to overcome handicaps, and to battle discouragement and fear, is the knowledge that they are involved in a purpose that is bigger than themselves. Because losers lack the quiet inner strength and motivation that comes from a sense of purpose, they

Often Suffer From:

TGIF (Thank God it's Friday) blues

The consequences of constantly being late or absent from
    work

Emotional fatigue from keeping up with the pace of life

The emptiness of underachieving

Boredom, anxiety, and depression.

Perhaps this inner strength is what Albert Schweitzer, who gave up a lucrative medical practice to spend his life caring for the natives of Africa, referred to when he said: "We must all mutually share in the knowledge that our exis-tence only attains its true value when we have experienced in ourselves the truth of the declaration, 'He who loses his life shall find it.' "

If you want to develop a winner's attitude, the first step is to make a strong and permanent commitment to invest your life and talents only in those pursuits that deserve your best efforts.

STEP 2

Make a Strong and Irrevocable Commitment to Give All That You Have, and All That You Are, To Achieve Your Goals!

When asked the secret of his success, Charles Dickens said, "Whatever I have tried to do in life, I have tried with my heart to do well."

That's the difference between winners and losers. Losers do what is required of them or even less; but winners always do more than is required—and they do it with enthusiasm. Losers are always looking for an easy way out. But winners, having committed themselves to work only toward their chosen goals, roll up their sleeves and take on challenges as they come. The great philosopher Elbert Hubbard once said, "Folks who never do more than they get paid to do, never get paid for any more than they do." Edward Markham put it another way:

> *For all your days, prepare;*
> *And meet them ever alike;*
> *When you are the anvil, bear;*
> *When you are the hammer, strike.*

Losers see themselves as doing a job. Winners see themselves as a part of all humankind and their work as their contribution to a better world. George Bernard Shaw, the great

English playwright, put it this way:

> I am convinced that my life belongs to the whole community and as long as I live, it is my privilege to do for it whatever I can, for the harder I work the more I live. I rejoice in life for its own sake. Life is no brief candle for me. It is a sort of splendid torch which I got hold of for a moment, and I want to make it burn as brightly as I possibly can before turning it over to future generations.

What an attitude! Can you imagine life ever being boring, or work dull, for a person with such a spirit?

The winner accepts the fact that problems are only opportunities in disguise. To the winner, everything is opportunity. Edmund Burke declared:

> The battle of life is in most cases fought up hill, and to win it without a struggle is almost like winning it without honour. If there were no difficulties, there would be no success; if there were nothing to struggle for, there would be nothing to be achieved. Difficulties may intimidate the weak, but they act only as a wholesome stimulus to men of resolution and valor. All experience of life, indeed, serves to prove that the impediments thrown in the way of human advance-

ment may, for the most part, be overcome by steady good conduct, honest zeal, activity, perseverance, and, above all, by a determined resolution to surmount difficulties and to stand up manfully against misfortune.

Nothing Works Like Work. Much has been said about STP, LSD, and THC—the escape-from-reality drugs. However, a far more dangerous escape vehicle is much more widespread than these drugs. It is SFN, or SOMETHING FOR NOTHING. For many people, its temptation is almost irresistible. It is frighteningly habit-forming. It destroys self-reliance and self-respect, and, psychologically, it has the guilt-producing impact of receiving stolen goods.

No wonder a leading psychiatrist has said that America is one big identity crisis. To the normal person who wakes up in the morning with nothing useful to do, and with nowhere to go where he or she is needed, life becomes a nightmare out of which that person must make some sense—or go crazy.

Consider these evaluations of work by some of the all-time winners:

Don't be misled into believing that somehow the world owes you a living. The boy who believes that his parents, or the government, or anyone else owes him his livelihood and that he can collect it without

labour will wake up one day and find himself working for another boy who did not have that belief and,
therefore, earned the right to have others work for
him. — *David Sarnoff*

The common denominator for success is work. Without work, man loses his vision, his confidence and his
determination to achieve. — *John D. Rockefeller*

"It's 99% perspiration, and 1% inspiration," when
asked to explain his genius. — *Thomas A. Edison*

If people knew how hard I worked to get my
mastery, it wouldn't seem so wonderful after all.
— *Michelangelo*

A genius? Perhaps, but before I was a genius I was a
drudge. — *Paderewski*

All the genius I have is the fruit of labour.
— *Alexander Hamilton*

You may have the loftiest goals, the highest ideals, the
noblest dreams, but remember this, nothing works unless
you do!

Hang in There—No Matter What! Losers are sometimes known for the projects they start; but winners are

remembered by the projects they complete. B.C. Forbes, founder of *Forbes Magazine,* once said, "One worthwhile task carried to a successful conclusion is better than half-a-hundred half-finished tasks."

Take a Look at These Track Records:
Henry Ford failed and went broke five times before he finally succeeded.

Babe Ruth, considered by sports historians to be the greatest athlete of all time and famous for setting the home run record, also holds the record for strikeouts.

Winston Churchill did not become Prime Minister of England until he was 62, and then only after a lifetime of defeats and setbacks. His greatest contributions came when he was a "senior citizen."

Eighteen publishers turned down Richard Bach's 10,000-word story about a "soaring" seagull, "Jonathan Livingston Seagull," before Macmillan finally published it in 1970. By 1975 it had sold more than 7 million copies in the U.S. alone.

Richard Hooker worked for seven years on his humorous war novel, "M*A*S*H," only to have it rejected by 21 publishers before Morrow decided to publish it.

It became a runaway bestseller, spawning a block-busting movie and a highly successful television series.

In life's success formula, nothing can take the place of persistence. Talent will not; it is common to find unsuccessful men with outstanding ability. Opportunity will not; many bungle their best chances by dropping the ball too soon. Enthusiasm will not; with the lazy and impatient, it can vanish overnight. Perseverance and determination alone are indispensable when it comes to getting the job done.

If what you are doing is worth doing, hang in there until it is done!

Some Won't Understand, but That's Okay! There will always be critics and skeptics who, unwilling to try themselves, will ridicule and criticize the person who plods on despite the circumstances. Abraham Lincoln was called "a gorilla" and "a buffoon." He was labeled by one of his peers "an embarrassment to the republic." I'd tell you who those critics were, but nobody seems to remember their names.

How About These Remarks:

You're putting an alligator there instead of a shirt pocket? I
  can't believe it! Those are never going to sell!

No worries boss. Nobody's going to buy those little Japanese cars.

Who on earth would want six bottles of the same thing in a
  package with a handle on it?

Those tires sure look flat to me. What did you say they're
   called? Radials?
Watches with no hands? You're crazy!
Oh come on. Don't tell me they can put music on Scotch tape.

About the negative people who always look for something to
criticize, the late President Theodore Roosevelt said:

> It's not the critic who counts; not the man who points
> out how the strongman stumbled or where the doer of
> deeds could have done them better. The credit
> belongs to the man who is actually in the arena; who
> strives valiantly, who errs and comes short again and
> again, because there is no effort without error and
> shortcoming; who does actually try to do the deed;
> who knows the great enthusiasm, the great devotion,
> knows in the end the triumph of high achievement,
> and who, at the worst, if he fails, at least fails while
> daring greatly. Far better is it to dare mighty things, to
> win glorious triumphs even though checkered by fail-
> ure, than to rank with those poor spirits who neither
> enjoy nor suffer much because they live in the grey
> twilight that knows neither victory nor defeat.

If you would develop a winner's attitude, make a strong
and irrevocable commitment to give all that you have, and
all that you are, to achieve the goals you have selected.

STEP 3

Make a Strong Commitment to Reach Your Full Potential As a Human Being!

Decide, once and for all time, that you will be the best you can be at whatever you set out to do. Vince Lombardi, the legendary coach of the Green Bay Packers, once gave the following brief but inspiring talk to his team:

> After the cheers have died and the stadium is empty, after the headlines have been written and after you are back in the quiet of your own room and the Super Bowl ring has been placed on the dresser and all the pomp and fanfare has faded, the enduring things that are left are: the dedication to excellence, the dedication to victory, and the dedication to doing with our lives the very best we can to make the world a better place in which to live.

I choose to see myself, and all other humans, as the creative expression of a loving God. In my view, atheistic humanism is at best inadequate and at worst arrogant. The Book of Genesis says that God, the sovereign of the universe, breathed into our nostrils, and gave us life. In other words, each of us contains a part of the Divine. Only when we are committed to excellence can we begin to measure up to all that we were created to be. Only as we see humankind as the product of a Supreme Being can we explain those thousands of daily strivings that call us to become something we have not yet been—those urges to live up to the best within us.

As Emerson would say, only our Maker can lead and teach us what we can do better than anyone else. Only our creator knows the full potential He placed within us.

"Anyone can count the seeds in an apple, but only God can count the apples in a seed," said Dr. Robert Schuller.

If you want the kind of happiness and deep personal satisfaction out of life that circumstances cannot destroy, search until you find what you can do best, what no one could pay you enough money not to do, what you would gladly pay for the privilege of doing. Then to it with all that is within you.

Consider who you are! You were born for greatness, because you were born from greatness. Consider, for a moment, some of the unique capabilities you possess as a human being.

The Ability to Think. Of all the creatures on the earth, only humans have such an enormous capacity to think, to reason, to store massive amounts of knowledge, to develop wisdom, to evaluate, and to view information in a variety of combinations. Yet scientists tell us that even the geniuses, like Einstein, Socrates, and Edison, used less than 10% of their mental capacities. As you reach out to develop your full potential, here are some tips that can help you unlock your tremendous mental powers:

Keep your mind uncluttered. Practice ridding your mind

of all negative, self-defeating thoughts.

Practice mental alertness. Your mind grows with exercise. Keep your mental radar working full time.

Cultivate your reasoning powers. Make a game of putting what you know into new combinations.

Feed your mind. Read, listen, and observe everything you can. Always make sure that you understand your mental input.

Cultivate curiosity. Ask questions about things you don't understand. Never be satisfied with what you know. Develop your imagination.

Organize your thoughts. Practice going from what you know, to discover what you don't know.

Be open. Never dismiss an idea as useless. Listen to viewpoints that are different from yours. You can learn something from every person you meet.

Practice Objectivity. Always be willing to examine an idea or bit of information from a variety of viewpoints.

Discipline your mind to work for you. Make it do what you want it to do, when you want it to do it.

Cultivate common sense. True wisdom is in knowing what to do with what you know. Learn to balance everything you know against the values that have meaning to you.

"I know of no more encouraging fact," said Thoreau, "than the fact that thought is a sculptor who can create the person you want to be."

The Ability to Create. The human mind, coupled with an

indomitable spirit and a marvelous physical body, is capable of creating in a way that is unknown anywhere in the universe. Even when the physical body is limited in certain key areas, the human mind and spirit can break free to create in the most amazing ways.

Consider Helen Keller. Born blind, deaf, and mute, she was cut off from the most vital links of communication with all other humans. Yet her keen mind and unconquerable spirit enabled her to write 27 books, as well as to inspire people all over the world to become more than they were.

If you would reach your full potential, cultivate all of the creative urges within you, and respond to the sensitivity that cries out for expression. Develop your best and most useful skills to their maximum level.

The greatest enemy of your creative powers is smug complacency—being satisfied with less than what you are capable of doing. In St. Peter's Cathedral, in Rome, there is an incredibly life-like statue of Moses. On one knee of that statue is a chip in the stone. Asked how it got there, a guide explained that it was placed there in frustration by the sculptor, Michelangelo. When the sculptor had finished his work, he looked tearfully at the statue, threw his hammer, and screamed, "Why dost thou not speak?"

Of course, no one ever becomes perfect, but anyone can improve. This urge to create, and to improve our creative abilities, gives us our best reason to grow—and to keep growing.

The Ability to Love. Human beings have both an overwhelming capacity to love and an overriding need to love and be loved. We need to reach out and to get into touch with other human beings. This urge expresses itself as soon as we draw our first breath, and it remains a part of our makeup until we draw our last breath.

Of all the human abilities, love is the most noble and the most ennobling. It is by far the most powerful force in the universe. Love moves the spirit to create, the mind to think, and the body to perform. Hate may be a strong force, as are self-centered egotism and fear. However, nothing can lift you to the heights enjoyed by those who respond to the love within and the love from others. Only love can make all your success worthwhile. Whatever else you cultivate, cultivate love. Only when you love and are loved can you reach your full potential as a human being.

The Ability to Laugh and Cry. As far as we know, humans are the only animals in the universe with the delicate emotional structure that enables them to laugh and to cry. To reach our full potential we need to do both. "A merry heart doeth good like a medicine: but a broken spirit drieth the bones," says the writer of Proverbs.

Experts on stress point out that a good sense of humor is a strong defense against being overcome by tension. The person who can laugh often, and who finds humor in even the most stressful events, can keep going when others are falling beside the way. People enjoy being around those who have a good sense of humor.

Weeping is also a part of the human experience. The loss of a loved one, the agony of defeat, severe disappointments, and many other circumstances bring sorrow to all of us. The key to emotional health is to learn how to handle grief. The person who reacts to sorrow only with anger becomes embittered, hardened, and cynical. Someone has said that tears wash the soul. I like the way Harry Emerson Fosdick put it: "Life asks not merely what can you do; it asks how much can you endure and not be spoiled." It was a wise old sage who said, "Life is a grindstone: whether it grinds you down or polishes you up depends on what you are made of."

We often quote the first part of Ella Wilcox's poem, "Laugh and the world laughs with you." But the remaining lines offer an important reminder about how to deal with sorrow and pain:

> *Weep, and you weep alone;*
> *For the sad old earth must borrow its mirth;*
> *But has trouble enough of its own.*

Laughter is a gift to be shared with all, but tears can best be endured alone—or with a friend who willingly shares our grief.

The Ability to Make Ethical and Moral Judgments. Other animals respond to innate drives, but humans have the capacity to make ethical and moral judgments. Call it conscience, values, or whatever you will, something in all of us rises up at times and says, "This is good!" or "This is bad!" And we ignore it at our own peril.

William Faulkner once gave some very good advice to a student: "I have found that the greatest help in meeting any problem with decency and self-respect and whatever courage is demanded is to know where you yourself stand. That is, to have in words what you believe and are acting from."

Ideas about morality are constantly changing, and the ways of coming to those moral judgments have been discussed in countless books. It is such a complex subject that many people simply choose not to face up to what it means to them. However, even that option is a moral judgment.

The Ability to Receive and Leave Behind a Heritage. Animals have to start from scratch with nothing but what they have inherited through their genes. A glorious part of the creative genius of humans, however, is that we have the ability to transmit knowledge and wisdom from one generation to the next. Humans have that unique ability to make their lives better by building on the vast storehouse of wisdom and knowledge that has come down to us through the ages. A few minutes at a public library can open to you the wisdom of the philosophers, to the romance of the poets, or to the knowledge of the scientists—even from centuries ago. Isn't it nice to know that you don't have to reinvent the wheel, rediscover fire, or develop a language? It is humbling to realize that most of the products of our lifetime are possible only because of the strivings and creative genius of those who have gone before us.

It is equally humbling to realize that what we do today will affect the lives of people for centuries to come. We, in turn, can pass along to our children, and to others, that which we have learned.

If you would reach your full potential as a human being, gratefully accept the heritage of the past, build on the wisdom of the ages for the present, and resolve to leave the world a better place than you found it.

How do you develop a winner's attitude? Make these three vital commitments and, having made them, renew them with every new day!

Make a strong and permanent commitment to invest your life and talents only in those pursuits that deserve your best efforts!

Make a strong and irrevocable commitment to give all that you have, and all that you are, to achieve your goals!

Make a strong commitment to reach your full potential as a human being!

Remember the words of Adlai E. Stevenson: "So live—decently, fearlessly, joyously—and don't forget that in the long run it is not the years in your life but the life in your years that counts."

CHAPTER 23

You Can Live An Amazing Life

IF YOU CAN DREAM IT, you can do it! But first you must *dare* to dream it. Contemplate the impossible. Remember the toughest thing that Sir Edmund Hillary had to confront before climbing Everest? Check the back jacket of this book.

Dare not only to dream, but dare to act on your dreams— to pursue your goals, your dreams and your visions. Action with a plan makes the wildest dreams come true!

You are born with inherited seeds of greatness. But these seeds, *all* seeds need to be nurtured to turn them into the blooms that we love so much. Every single day the seeds of your potential greatness need to be tended to bring out the best of your personality, your creativity, and your qualities of leadership. And pursuing the metaphor one more time? Without fertilizer, the fruits of your potential greatness will die on the vine. Absolutely guaranteed.

Dare to do what?

Dare to start a business.
Dare to finish university.
Dare to get married.
Dare to have children.
Dare to serve your community.
Dare to fail.
Dare to change.
Dare to be a winner.
Dare to start new projects.
Dare to be creative.
Dare to believe in God.
Dare to love unconditionally.
Dare to succeed.
Dare to set goals.
Dare to chart a new course.
Dare to have an amazing life.

If my list is not long enough to get you started, add more dares of your own!

To finish up, here's a story about a man who dared—who went the impossible distance from commanding a slave ship to Christian ministry—and in the process, left us a stirring legacy. It is a story retold from a variety of sources, but I will give most of the credit to a gentleman called Al Rogers, who put it together for a publication called *Away Here in Texas.* I found it on the Web, and have paraphrased and condensed some of Mr. Rogers' splendid and detailed narrative.

In 1736, at the age of 11, John Newton went to sea with his father, the commander of a merchant ship that sailed the Mediterranean. In 1744, following the death of his father, John was pressed into service on *H.M.S. Harwich,* but finding conditions intolerable, he deserted. Soon recaptured, he was publicly flogged and demoted to common seaman.

In due course, he entered service on a slave ship, which took him to the coast of Sierra Leone. He then became the servant of a slave trader and was brutally abused, before being rescued by a sea captain who had known John's father. John Newton ultimately became captain of his own slave trader.

Although he had had some early religious instruction from his mother, Newton had long since given up any religious convictions. However, on a homeward voyage, attempting to steer his ship through a violent storm, he experienced what he was to refer to later as his "great deliverance." He recorded in his journal that when all seemed lost and the ship would surely sink, he exclaimed, "Lord, have mercy upon us!" Later in his cabin he reflected on what he had said and began to believe that God had addressed him through the storm, that grace had begun to work for him.

For the rest of his life he observed the anniversary of May 10, 1748, as the day of his conversion, a day of humiliation in which he subjected his will to a higher power. He continued in the slave trade for a time after his conversion, but saw to it that the slaves under his care were treated humanely.

By 1755, after a serious illness, he had given up seafaring forever, and from 1755 to 1760, Newton was surveyor of tides at Liverpool, where he came to know George Whitefield, deacon in the Church of England, evangelistic preacher, and leader of the Calvinistic Methodist Church. Newton decided to become a minister, and applied to the Archbishop of York for ordination. The Archbishop refused his request, but Newton persisted, and was subsequently ordained by the Bishop of Lincoln and accepted the curacy of Olney, in Buckinghamshire. Newton's church became so crowded during services that it had to be enlarged. He preached not only in Olney but also in other parts of the country. In 1767 the poet William Cowper settled at Olney, and he and Newton became friends.

Cowper helped Newton with his religious services and on his tours to other places. They held not only a regular weekly church service but also began a series of weekly prayer meetings, for which their goal was to write a new hymn for each one. They collaborated on several editions of *Olney Hymns,* which achieved lasting popularity.

Among Newton's contributions was Amazing Grace, possibly one of the hymns written for a weekly service. Through the years other writers have composed additional verses to the hymn, but these are the six stanzas that appeared, with minor spelling variations, in both the first Olney edition in 1779 and the 1808 edition, the one nearest the date of Newton's death.

Al Rogers says that the origin of the melody is unknown, but most hymnals attribute it to an early American folk melody. The Bill Moyers PBS special on Amazing Grace speculated that it might have originated as the tune of a song the slaves sang.

In 1780 Newton left Olney to become rector of St. Mary Woolchurch in London. There he drew large congregations and influenced many, among them William Wilberforce, who would one day become a leader in the campaign for the abolition of slavery. Newton continued to preach until the last year of his life, although he was blind by that time. He died in London on December 21, 1807.

There is an expression something like: "When the student is ready, the teacher will come." Often quite miraculously! A storm was the dramatic catalyst that would change the life of John Newton, who would, in turn, change the life of William Wilberforce. Amazing Grace became a hymn that reflected Newton's salvation, and today, whenever we hear it, it stirs us with its message of hope.

In this book you have read my stories about people who dared and won—philanthropist and friend Joe Segal, Morris Wosk, Peter Armstrong, Wendy Lisogar-Cocchia, shoeshiner Shed, Rubin "Hurricane" Carter, Grace McCarthy, Maurice "Rocket" Richard, Mike Dosen, astronaut Julie Payette, Jackie Gleason and many others.

The list is a work in progress. And so too is your life.

Amazing grace! (How sweet the sound)
That sav'd a wretch like me!
I once was lost, but now am found,
Was blind, but now I see.

'Twas grace that taught my heart to fear,
And grace my fears reliev'd;
How precious did that grace appear,
The hour I first believ'd!

Thro' many dangers, toils and snares,
I have already come;
'Tis grace has brought me safe thus far,
And grace will lead me home.

The Lord has promis'd good to me,
His word my hope secures;
He will my shield and portion be,
As long as life endures.

Yes, when this flesh and heart shall fail,
And mortal life shall cease;
I shall possess, within the veil,
A life of joy and peace.

The earth shall soon dissolve like snow,
The sun forbear to shine;
But God, who call'd me here below,
Will be forever mine.

About the Author

PETER LEGGE
CSP • CPAE

"Inspirational!" "Spellbinding!" "The best ever!"

FROM NEW YORK TO LOS ANGELES, from Frankfurt to the Philippines, audiences reach for superlatives to describe the presentations of Peter Legge. Filled with stuff that reaches the heart, with words that move and motivate, Peter's keynote addresses and seminars are nothing short of spectacular.

Peter is President and CEO of Canada Wide Magazines and Communications Ltd., the largest independently owned publishing company in Western Canada—with a network of 20 magazines, and annual sales in excess of $25 million.

Peter travels the world as a motivational speaker, accepting more than 100 assignments each year from clients who know that when he speaks, his words will be a catalyst for positive change.

In company with very few others, Toastmasters International has awarded Peter the Golden Gavel, and honored him as Top Speaker in North America. He is also a Certified Speaking Professional, a proudly earned designation of the National Speakers Association.

Peter is tireless in his commitment to the community. Among his good works, he is a Director of Variety Club of British Columbia and a Variety Club International Ambassador.

As a successful businessman, community leader, father and husband, Peter's wry observations on life are crafted into powerful messages. He has told many of his stories in four best-selling books—*How To Soar With The Eagles, You Can If You Believe You Can, It Begins With A Dream,* and *If Only I'd Said That.* He also has released a two-cassette audio album *25 Success Secrets,* a tremendous reinforcement of the motivational message.

Peter is topical, on target—and guaranteed great!

OTHER INSPIRATIONAL BOOKS
FOR YOUR PERSONAL LIBRARY

Please call Janice Maxwell at 604-299-7311

4th Floor, 4180 Lougheed Hwy

Burnaby, B.C. V5C 6A7

Canada

or e-mail plegge@canadawide.com

ORDER FORM

No	Description	Qty	Price	Total
B100	Who Dares Wins *Hard Cover*		29.95 CDN 25.95 U.S.	
B101	If Only I'd Said That *Hard Cover*		29.95 CDN 25.95 U.S.	
B102	It Begins With A Dream *Hard Cover*		29.95 CDN 25.95 U.S.	
B103	You Can If You Believe You Can *Hard Cover*		25.95 CDN 19.95 U.S.	
B104	How To Soar With The Eagles *Hard Cover*		25.95 CDN 19.95 U.S.	
	VIDEOTAPES			
V101	How To Soar With The Eagles (90 mins.)		30.00 CDN 25.00 U.S.	
V102	"Live" in Orlando (60 mins.)		30.00 CDN 25.00 U.S.	
	AUDIOTAPES			
A101	25 Success Secrets (90 mins.)		30.00 CDN 25.00 U.S.	
A102	A Tribute to Fathers (53 mins.)		20.00 CDN 15.00 U.S.	
	SUBTOTAL			
	SHIPPING AND HANDLING		5.00 CDN 3.00 U.S.	
	SUBTOTAL			
	CANADIAN RESIDENTS ADD 7% GST			
	BC RESIDENTS ADD 7% PST (TAPES ONLY)			
	TOTAL			

For faster service FAX your credit card order to **(604) 299-9188**
or call **(604) 299-7311**

PAYMENT

☐ Cheque payable to Peter Legge Management Co. Ltd.

☐ Please charge $_____ to my MasterCard/Visa

CC# _____Expiry Date_____

Signature _____

Please send my order to: (Please print)

Name_____

Address_____

City_____Prov/State _____Postal/Zip_____

Peter Legge Management Co. Ltd., 4th Floor, 4180 Lougheed Hwy., Burnaby, B.C. V5C 6A7 Canada